Big Bear

SERIES EDITOR:
John Ralston Saul

Big Bear

by RUDY WIEBE

With an Introduction by
John Ralston Saul
SERIES EDITOR

EXTRAORDINARY
CANADIANS

Mississippi Mills Public Library

PENGUIN CANADA

Published by the Penguin Group

Penguin Group (Canada), 90 Eglinton Avenue East, Suite 700, Toronto,
Ontario, Canada M4P 2Y3 (a division of Pearson Canada Inc.)

Penguin Group (USA) Inc., 375 Hudson Street, New York, New York 10014, U.S.A.
Penguin Books Ltd, 80 Strand, London WC2R 0RL, England
Penguin Ireland, 25 St Stephen's Green, Dublin 2, Ireland
(a division of Penguin Books Ltd)
Penguin Group (Australia), 250 Camberwell Road, Camberwell, Victoria 3124, Australia
(a division of Pearson Australia Group Pty Ltd)
Penguin Books India Pvt Ltd, 11 Community Centre, Panchsheel Park,
New Delhi – 110 017, India
Penguin Group (NZ), 67 Apollo Drive, Rosedale, North Shore 0745, Auckland,
New Zealand (a division of Pearson New Zealand Ltd)
Penguin Books (South Africa) (Pty) Ltd, 24 Sturdee Avenue, Rosebank,
Johannesburg 2196, South Africa

Penguin Books Ltd, Registered Offices: 80 Strand, London WC2R 0RL, England

First published 2008

1 2 3 4 5 6 7 8 9 10 (RRD)

Copyright © Jackpine House Ltd., 2008
Introduction copyright © John Ralston Saul, 2008

Manufactured in the U.S.A.

LIBRARY AND ARCHIVES CANADA CATALOGUING IN PUBLICATION

Wiebe, Rudy, 1934–
Big Bear/Rudy Wiebe.

(Extraordinary Canadians)
Includes bibliographical references.
ISBN 978-0-670-06786-2

1. Big Bear, 1825?–1888. 2. Cree Indians—Prairie Provinces—History.
3. Cree Indians—Kings and rulers—Biography. 4. Cree Indians—Prairie Provinces—
Biography. 5. Indians of North Amercia—Prairie Provinces—Biography.
6. Indians of North America—Prairie Provinces—History. I. Title. II. Series.

E99.C88B5 2008   971.2004973230092   C2008-902622-5

Visit the Penguin Group (Canada) website at **www.penguin.ca**

Special and corporate bulk purchase rates available; please see
www.penguin.ca/corporatesales or call 1-800-810-3104, ext. 477 or 474

This book was printed on 30% PCW recycled paper

Dedicated to the memory of

See-as-cum-ka-poo (Little Stones on the Prairie) also
  known as Mary PeeMee
and John Tootoosis
and Duncan McLean

  who told me Big Bear stories

And to Gil Cardinal, who made the movie

CONTENTS

John Ralston Saul

How do civilizations imagine themselves? One way is for each of us to look at ourselves through our society's most remarkable figures. I'm not talking about hero worship or political iconography. That is a danger to be avoided at all costs. And yet people in every country do keep on going back to the most important people in their past.

This series of Extraordinary Canadians brings together rebels, reformers, martyrs, writers, painters, thinkers, political leaders. Why? What is it that makes them relevant to us so long after their deaths?

For one thing, their contributions are there before us, like the building blocks of our society. More important than that are their convictions and drive, their sense of what is right and wrong, their willingness to risk all, whether it be their lives, their reputations, or simply being wrong in public. Their ideas, their triumphs and failures, all of these somehow constitute a mirror of our society. We look at these people, all dead, and discover what we have been, but also what we can be. A mirror is an instrument for measuring ourselves. What we see can be both a warning and an encouragement.

These eighteen biographies of twenty key Canadians are centred on the meaning of each of their lives. Each of them is very different, but these are not randomly chosen great figures. Together they produce a grand sweep of the creation of modern Canada, from our first steps as a democracy in 1848 to our questioning of modernity late in the twentieth century.

All of them except one were highly visible on the cutting edge of their day while still in their twenties, thirties, and forties. They were young, driven, curious. An astonishing level of fresh energy surrounded them and still does. We in the twenty-first century talk endlessly of youth, but power today is often controlled by people who fear the sort of risks and innovations embraced by everyone in this series. A number of them were dead—hanged, infected on a battlefield, broken by their exertions—well before middle age. Others hung on into old age, often profoundly dissatisfied with themselves.

Each one of these people has changed you. In some cases you know this already. In others you will discover how through these portraits. They changed the way the world hears music, thinks of war, communicates. They changed how each of us sees what surrounds us, how minorities are treated, how we think of immigrants, how we look after each other, how we imagine ourselves through what are now our stories.

You will notice that many of them were people of the word. Not just the writers. Why? Because civilizations are built around many themes, but they require a shared public language. So Laurier, Bethune, Douglas, Riel, LaFontaine, McClung, Trudeau, Lévesque, Big Bear, even Carr and Gould, were masters of the power of language. Beaverbrook was one of the most powerful newspaper publishers of his day. Countries need action and laws and courage. But civilization is not a collection of prime ministers. Words, words, words—it is around these that civilizations create and imagine themselves.

The authors I have chosen for each subject are not the obvious experts. They are imaginative, questioning minds from among our leading writers and activists. They have, each one of them, a powerful connection to their subject. And in their own lives, each is engaged in building what Canada is now becoming.

That is why a documentary is being filmed around each subject. Images are yet another way to get at each subject and to understand their effect on us.

There has not been a biographical project as ambitious as this in a hundred years, not since the Makers of Canada series.

And yet every generation understands the past differently, and so sees in the mirror of these remarkable figures somewhat different lessons.

What strikes me again and again is just how dramatically ethical decisions figured in their lives. They form the backbone of history and memory. Some of these people, Big Bear, for example, or Dumont, or even Lucy Maud Montgomery, thought of themselves as failures by the end of their lives. But the ethical cord that was strung taut through their work has now carried them on to a new meaning and even greater strength, long after their deaths.

Each of these stories is a revelation of the tough choices unusual people must make to find their way. And each of us as readers will find in the desperation of the Chinese revolution, the search for truth in fiction, the political and military dramas, different meanings that strike a personal chord. At first it is that personal emotive link to such figures which draws us in. Then we find they are a key that opens the whole society of their time to us. Then we realize that in that 150-year period many of them knew each other, were friends, opposed each other. Finally, when all these stories are put together, you will see that a whole new debate has been created around Canadian civilization and the shape of our continuous experiment.

The full meaning of that continuity comes out with Big Bear. We have slowly convinced ourselves that this country can be explained through European traditions. It cannot. To do so is a betrayal of our own past. We cannot grow as a civilization by trying to push the Aboriginal reality to the margins. For example, I cannot think of another powerful leader in the history of Canada who so consciously and publicly lived by ethical decisions; the kind of ethical standards we would like to attach to our society today. Through all his dramas he never ceased trying to explain the difference between what today we would call the public good versus self-interest.

You can look upon his life as a long and tragic defeat. Or you can look upon Big Bear as an illustration of what is best in our civilization. An ethical leader who suffers tragedy and defeat will often become a model for those who follow.

Rudy Wiebe tells Big Bear's story in that great, dramatic tradition. For much of Canada, the latter part of the nineteenth century saw unbridled land hunger and political ambition tear the country apart. From that confusion Big Bear emerges—calm, ironic, coolly angry, always ready to explain—as one who can show us the way, thanks to his actions and to his words.

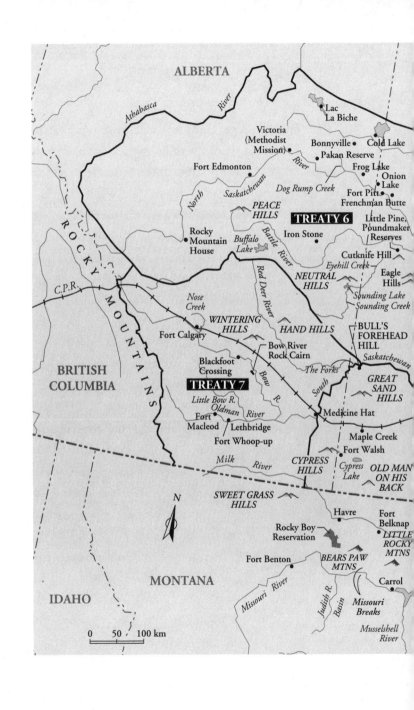

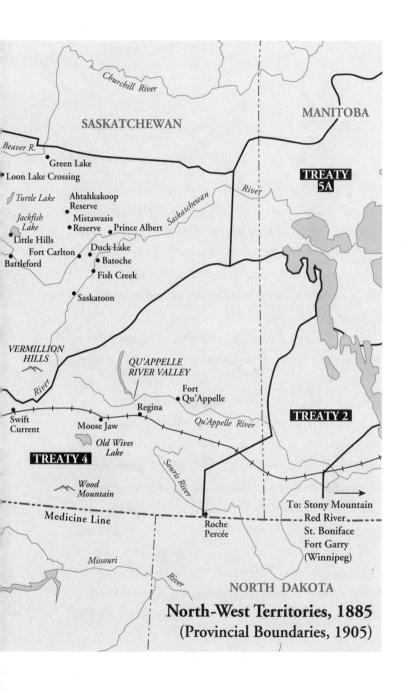

North-West Territories, 1885
(Provincial Boundaries, 1905)

How can you write the story of a nineteenth-century man who lived within the oral, hunting culture of Plains Cree and Saulteaux? Whose magnificent orations were never written down in his richly metaphorical languages, who spoke no English, and whose profound, extended images exist only in bits of translation—often made by incompetent translators— that were recorded largely by his enemies?

To try to write Big Bear's story, I researched beyond the standard, accepted facts of White Canadian history and considered carefully the complex Plains Cree culture and the enormous physical landscape in which Big Bear lived. His known actions speak to his character and wisdom, his constant spiritual beliefs. The most reliable written records of his words are the few he dictated in Cree to the English speakers he could (or had to) trust. Some of his more sympathetic recorders (e.g., William Cameron, William McLean) understood minimal Cree, and some of his most prejudiced (e.g., P.G. Laurie, David Laird) knew none whatever, so I have relied most heavily on the sparse testimony of fluent Cree speakers (e.g., James Simpson, Peter Erasmus, Henry Halpin). But even more important than these written accounts were the oral tradition accounts recorded by

Cree Elders, whose living memories of what their ancestors (Big Bear's contemporaries) told them have carried his powerful story into the present. I found those oral accounts given in Stonechild and Waiser, McLeod, Dempsey, and O-sak-do especially informative (see "Sources").

Nevertheless, for me much of Big Bear remained beyond the rational grasp of terse, noun-dominated English. The fluidity of verb and metaphor, something of the sustained poetry, the physical orality of *Cree* was needed. And perhaps written English could approach that through intimate conversation, could find that spiritual place where land and friendship offer us the optic power of the audible heart.

So, using the characters and places that history provides, I have also written short dramatic scenes that no history before the invention of the motion-picture camera could possibly record. Big Bear's long friendship with Hudson's Bay Company trader James Keith Simpson—a Scots-Cree man of his own age—gave me the idea. During his cross-examination as a witness at Big Bear's trial in 1885, Simpson stated that he had known the chief for "nearly forty years" and that he "was into [Big Bear's] camp often trading with them, summer and winter, the same as if I was living with them altogether."

Please note that, to keep matters clear, in these invented (and, in that sense, timeless) conversations I do not use speaker quotation marks. However, all the recorded statements/conversations I quote, whether from oral or written sources, are cited accurately within double quotation marks in both the text and block quotes. The speakers/writers are identified in context.

CHAPTER ONE

Buffalo; Guns and Horses

This story happened more than a century ago, but it is still going on. If you want to know it, read this book and then watch the television news or read a newspaper. The news stories about First Nations in Canada today echo the life lived by Big Bear and other Plains Cree in what is now called Saskatchewan, Alberta, and Montana. Big Bear was both more ancient and more modern than the nineteenth-century White Canadians who tried to destroy him. His innate conviction that he had the human right to be himself was as powerful as his understanding of his inalienable right to the land that had sustained and protected his ancestors for five hundred generations.

THERE ONCE WAS A BABY BOY born at Jackfish Lake, near present-day North Battleford, Saskatchewan, who would grow up to receive the Cree name Mistahimaskwa, Big Bear. His father was Mukatai, Black Powder, a Saulteaux who had long been chief of a Plains Cree band, and his mother was either Cree or Saulteaux. Her name was perhaps too powerful to speak aloud, because no one can remember it. Her name is simply given as None. In the same way, sixty years later, on September 29, 1885, the Inmate Admittance Records of Stony Mountain Penitentiary will declare Big Bear's religion to be None. And there his name will vanish as well. In a tiny cell inside stone walls as impenetrable as the limestone cliffs they are built upon, Mistahimaskwa will become a number, Prisoner 103, until he was discharged in February 1887. To die within a year.

Big Bear died in the lee of Cutknife Hill during a January snowstorm, not fifty kilometres as the raven flies from the lake where he was born. As he explained to fellow Cree chiefs gathered near Fort Carlton in 1884: "Our People lived with the buffalo all our lives, so we were blind in regard to making treaty. We did not understand the treaty when we heard of it, nor saw what use we had for it. Our food and clothing were in our hands, the country was free to us wherever we wanted to go, that was why we thought ourselves rich."

And the land given to the First People by the Creator—the land stripped from them by treaty—is still very rich. There are again buffalo beside Jackfish Lake where Big Bear was born, herds of cows and bulls and yearlings and little tan calves. But now they graze behind seven strands of barbed wire.

It was because of the buffalo that many Woods Cree in the late eighteenth century moved to the edges of the boreal forest and gradually became powerful Plains People. As forest hunters they had begun a shrewd trade with the Hudson's Bay Company when ships from England first arrived in 1668. Beyond meeting their own want for goods such as kettles, needles, tobacco, and tea to gather hospitable groups around winter fires, the Cree quickly became the peaceful middlemen for other tribes far inland. An axe traded at Hudson Bay for one beaver was worth six beavers when carried a thousand miles inland by canoe to the buffalo-hunting Blackfoot Confederacy, who lived between the Saskatchewan rivers, or to the corn-growing Mandan along the Missouri; a fourteen-beaver gun was worth fifty.

However, with time, new political relations developed among the tribes, caused by both the pressure of woodland people pushing into prairie hunting territory and the arrival of the horse. While trading with the Cree for European goods, the Blackfoot began to accumulate horses from their southern neighbours. This conjunction on the Great Plains of convenient iron from the north—particularly steel knives and guns—with the astounding strength of horses from the south transformed everyone's way of hunting the buffalo that grazed everywhere to the prairie horizon. The huge animals that offered everything needed for life, for health and happiness, now no longer needed to be hunted in a solitary, dangerous stalk; People no longer needed to build complex lanes to lure and drive buffalo over the cliffs of a killing jump, or into the corralled surround of a pound, where their wild strength could be crushed together into immobility and speared to death. A horse could outrun any buffalo, it could bring its mounted hunter so close, running flat-out, that one arrow behind the shoulder, one bullet, could drop the great animal dead in its tracks. And beyond that, huge, moveable communal hunts with their glorious camaraderie became not only possible, they also provided rich food for great numbers of People.

The Woods Cree recognized that if they joined into large bands on the plains for the summer and hunted the shifting herds, they could live well and also dry enough meat for pounded pemmican and tan enough hides for clothing and lodges to take them comfortably through the winter inside their familiar forests. Avoiding the isolated bush loneliness of small family groups stalking a solitary moose to survive the winter darkness, they could now enjoy year-round the comfort and safety of many People living together. All they needed was more horses.

Only the prairie Blackfoot Confederacy of Siksika, Blood, and Peigan could provide horses in numbers. Gradually their peaceful trading partnership turned into conflict. As the pressure for additional hunting space and horses grew, trading evolved into raids. Why trade when, if you were daring and clever enough, you could steal twenty Blackfoot horses in one night? To return home riding a magnificent buffalo runner and singing a personal song of triumph (and your opponent's humiliation) became a Cree warrior's high honour. The more horses you captured, the more horses you could give to your friends, the better you could all hunt, the more stories you could recite during communal festivals, and the more swiftly you could ride over hill and prairie, the wind whistling happiness in your ears.

By the mid-1820s, the peaceful trading partnership between Cree and Blackfoot was largely an Elder's memory. For decades the Horse Wars shaped both societies: endless repetitions of swift, brutal raids and short-lived peace treaties. After 1810, Hudson's Bay Company traders typically recorded events such as these: "Blackfoot warriors attacked a Beaver Hills Cree camp, destroying 16 tents," or "100 Cree warriors attacking a Blood camp of 30 lodges on the Red Deer River and killing a good many and bringing away 96 horses and six women." European trade goods had intensified conflict among communities over tribal territory.

The Plains Cree lived and hunted in loose, shifting bands following a senior, prestigious civil chief; in times of attack or emergency, a younger war chief took command and organized band response. An official crier would walk through camp, shouting the news of the day, the chief's orders, or the call to council. The council circle advised the chief about necessary decisions, the youngest men speaking first. But anyone, including women, could voice opinions until the chief made a, usually consensus, decision. In 1872, English officer William Butler (later The Right Honourable General Sir William Butler), commissioned by Prime Minister Macdonald to travel across the North-West, described the Cree society he encountered in this way:

> "[The Cree] who first welcomed the [White] new-comer is the only perfect socialist or communist in the world. He holds all things in common with his tribe—the land, the bison, the river…. He kills a moose and to the last bit the coveted food is shared by all…. If a stranger comes and he is hungry, let him be first served and best attended to. If one child starves in an Indian camp, you may know that in every lodge every stomach is hungry."

Butler's colonial-romantic style describes an historic reality. The last quarter of the nineteenth century would prove that such a communal hunting and gathering world of independent Peoples could not survive the relentless pressure of eastern Canada's agricultural and industrial society.

CHAPTER TWO

Plains Cree Boy

So in 1825, Big Bear was born at Jackfish Lake into a hunting horse-warrior band. His father, Black Powder, was chief of eighty mixed Plains Cree–Saulteaux People, and they were true nomadic hunters. They avoided the prairie Horse Wars and raiding as much as possible by wintering in the forests around Jackfish Lake and The Little Hills, trapping beaver and hunting moose. In spring they travelled to Fort Carlton on the North Saskatchewan River to trade their furs; in summer and autumn they followed the buffalo herds as far west as Buffalo Lake or south to the Red Deer River. Like many Woodland Saulteaux who moved onto the prairie, Black Powder was a powerful fighter, though he did not flaunt his warrior reputation and tried to avoid confrontation with the Blackfoot. He was widely known for his spiritual and medicine powers.

When Black Powder's son had grown enough to be taken out of his moss bag, the child ran through the summer days playing with other children, or puppies, or grass or sand or in lake or stream water. He could do whatever he pleased in the complete world of his parents' camp, wander into any group of women working, into any lodge or council circle. He could even enter the sacred Thirst Dance Lodge and sway to the big drums' beat, the singers' ever-rising song. He wore nothing but a small pouch on a thong around his neck, which contained his umbilical cord and tobacco. When an Elder smiled at him, he might weave among the dancers to that Person, who would touch him and take a pinch of tobacco from the pouch and offer it to the Spirits in prayer for the boy. That could happen any day, in any season, a continual communal supplication for their chief's first-born son, even when he climbed through the lodge door after watching Sun flame down to rest below the circle of Earth. Inside the lodge was a blue fire of buffalo chips behind which Black Powder sat, thinking, and People talked around him, the lodge a great cone of light drifting through the rising smoke of laughter. The boy would snuggle down to a story.

"Here is another one, from long ago. Wîsahkêcâhk the trickster was walking around, and he saw young partridges in a nest. My little brothers, partridges, what is your name? But you just named us, they cried, when you said partridges. That is the only name we have. No, said Wîsahkêcâhk. Everything has two names. No, they told him, we have only this name, partridges. No, little brothers! Think, you have some other name too. Finally the oldest one said, It's true, our mother does say to us Little Startlers, and Partridges, too. Yes, we do have two names. Acchh, Wîsahkêcâhk told them sarcastically, you couldn't startle anybody! You're so little, you...."

The little boy is thinking what his second name might be. Will he ever startle anyone? He will think about his name through all of Wîsahkêcâhk's other tricks and blunders, when he is chased by a rolling stone and it begins to crawl up his leg—but by the time the storyteller says, This is the end of this sacred story, the little boy is curled among the hides close against his warm mother, far away in sleep.

Life shifted when the boy was seven. A mentor began to teach him a Cree's necessary knowledge: how to ride, how to use the bow and knife, how to see distance and distinguish between the dust of buffalo and a wisp of Blackfoot smoke while lying on a prairie hill, how moose could stand submerged to their nostrils in forest sloughs, how the entrances of beaver lodges hid under water. The year he was eight, starvation slowly stalked all the northern prairie People through the winter until in spring heavy snowstorms drove Black Powder's band into dying. There were no buffalo; the Company trader at Carlton reported he had seen none for more than nine months and had no food himself. So they had to move quickly south, deeper than ever into Blackfoot country, beyond The Forks of the South Saskatchewan and Red Deer rivers to the Great Sand Hills. Why had the animals gone so far away? It almost seemed a threat: we will never return north.

And there was worse to come, in the south. Smallpox, the invisible enemy that could not be fought; it could only be run away from. In the spring of 1837, smallpox came in a White boat up the Missouri River and destroyed most of the Mandan People; of 1,000 Assiniboine only 150 survived, and it spread from them west and north through the Blackfoot and Cree bands on the plains. Flight, horrifying sickness, death: two-thirds of the Blackfoot Confederacy died, while the Cree fled, scattering into the boreal forest. Whole circles of lodges with rotting bodies were left for prairie vultures and wolves.

Black Powder's band was badly infected. His oldest son also became desperately ill, but unlike so many, the twelve-year-old boy did not die. He had the strength and spirit to endure the dreadful pain in his head, neck, and back; the almost unstoppable bleeding of his nose; and the agonizing red pustules that erupted over his head and body. Eventually they ruptured into stinking pus, and he began to recover. When after two months he could walk again, the once-perfect skin of his face was disfigured by scars, deep pits that would shift and fold with age but never be gone.

On an autumn evening Black Powder helped his son walk out into the prairie air. The grass swished like slow breathing against their moccasins. The stinging whine of mosquitoes had disappeared, and in the silence they heard the bellow of buffalo bulls, far away. From beside a pond came the chitter of prairie chicken hens running in the long files of their autumn dance as the cocks drummed to their echo: *boom boom booooo!* For a moment the boy could not control his hands: they touched the scars on his ravaged face, then dropped to his sides.

I'm lucky, he said. I'll always be behind it, I'll never have to look at my face!

Black Powder laughed aloud with him. Yes, he said. And everyone who does look will know, instantly, that your Spirit medicine power is stronger than the worst White disease.

But this White "present" made me so sick....

Yes, said his father, and that proved your medicine power. You will always have more, the White stinking disease can never kill you now.

That winter the boy's voice, so quick for laughter and stories, began to deepen. The following summer, when the band was again hunting near The Forks, in the darkness of early morning Black Powder paddled his son across the South Saskatchewan River. Together they walked through the valley cottonwoods and climbed up the slopes and knobby bends of Bull's Forehead Hill. When they reached the top, they saw the circle of the earth beginning to brighten, saw where the two rivers joined into one to curl east toward the light and the grass spread away under the coming sun to a southern ripple of Great Sand Hills. Together they erected stick frameworks and hung offerings on them, red cloth and patterned brown and yellow. They set the buffalo skull under the shelter and spread the bearskin; then his father offered up a pipe and left him.

The boy saw Sun rise over the rim of Earth, and he faced Him all day. Praying for vision, crying out and lifting his arms in supplication when it seemed he could no longer stand in the fierce light of the endless summer day. Stripped to a breechcloth, his feet in the bear fur, he stared over the prairie and the long bend of the South Saskatchewan and the valley hills folded down like green blankets until Sun sank at last into the bloody loops of the Red Deer River and he could collapse.

On the second day he did not stand, nor move. He was not hungry; thirst tried to break his concentration. He did not look at the point where the two rivers merged and bent away together. He wept and prayed, and at night spirits began to come. Not one, many—but he refused them. Bear spirits came, and he would not listen to them either. He fasted and prayed into the third day, with not a cloud in the burning sky to grant him a drop of rain, until finally out of his accepted suffering the overlord of all bear spirits came: the Great Parent of Bear reared up over him with his arms wide and fangs bared, growling dreadfully. Then He dropped down to become what the Cree also called Him: Four-legged Person. From dry ground Bear scooped up wet clay and clawed it over the boy's face in five great slashes, taught him his vision song and the words of it:

"My teeth are my knives,
My claws are my knives."

And he instructed him how to make the core of his sacred bundle. All his life, this sacred object was to be his sign that his prayer had been answered, that, under the Creator, the most powerful Spirit known to his People had come, and would come again, to help him whenever he prayed for guidance and strength, especially in war.

Big Bear named the core of his bundle Chief's Son's Hand and made it as it was revealed to him in his vision quest. He skinned out a giant bear paw very long, with its five enormous claws still attached, and with buffalo thongs sewed the paw onto a piece of scarlet stroud. Then he cut the cloth into a bib, so that when he tied it around his neck with thongs, the black fur would wrap round his neck like a scarf and the paw with the great ivory claws rested below the hollow of his throat. The Cree understand that a person's soul is given to them at birth and resides along the back of the neck, and so, when Big Bear had offered up all the sacred ceremonies and tied the thongs around his neck and felt the weight of Chief's Son's Hand warm against his soul, he knew himself to be in perfect, assured communion with the Great Parent of Bear. He had Bear power.

After each prayer ceremony and wearing of the neckpiece, he would wrap the paw in a new gift of cloth, place the bundle inside a tanned leather bag, and store it carefully. The whole object—Chief's Son's Hand, wrapping cloths, and bag—was called *That Which Is Kept In A Clean Place*.

And his name was now Mistahi Maskwa. *Maskwa* meaning "bear," but *mistahi* in particular, so together meaning

"Much ... or A-Whole-Lot-Of Bear." Which, upon contemplation, could shape-shift into More-Than-Enough Bear. For Whites of course, and their frozen English comprehension of names, he would simply be Big Bear.

CHAPTER THREE

Warrior and Chief

Big Bear was growing into a Young Man; he would now ceremonially unwrap the cloths around Chief's Son's Hand and wear it around his neck for protection in a horse raid or war or to defend his camp. He became a renowned warrior; the stories of his exploits against the Blackfoot are still remembered and retold by his great-great-grandchildren.

But the mystic power of Chief's Son's Hand also came to him as a gift when he contemplated his People living, when he walked among the spring aspen or rode under the thunderheads of prairie sky—long thoughts that circled back as far as his faintest memory of the Elders' stories and into the shadows of what was coming. For if Whites they had never seen could destroy People with sickness, wipe them away like snow before a winter chinook and leave children with parents rotting before their eyes, the smell of death choking them while they barely knew whether they themselves were alive or dead—if Whites could do that from unseeable distances—what might they not do when they confronted his People in massive numbers? Like they already did south of the Medicine Line border, where forts contained not only a few traders with helpers but also packs of blue soldiers who marched around stiff-legged, carrying guns that ended in bright steel knives.

Enough eyes had seen them. Stories were told in every camp how some Plains Cree had been taken aboard a boat that sailed down the Missouri River and then up another and another until they rode wagons over mountains to a place of endless square houses called Washington and a man they called their Big White Father (President Andrew Jackson, 1832) hung silver medals around their necks. The next summer these Cree men came home with many gifts and more horses than they had left with, the silver medals still hanging from their necks.

There were no soldiers at Carlton or Pitt or Edmonton along the North Saskatchewan River, but there were "God-men" who said they spoke for the Great Spirit, men named Thibault and De Smet who wanted to be called Father and walked in their black dresses onto the prairie to the buffalo with the Métis and sometimes even visited the Plains Cree bands of Chief Sweetgrass to talk about water and spirit and blood. And now (1840) another God-man, named Rundle, had passed by upriver to Edmonton, and it was said that a Cree who once wore a silver medal, the renowned warrior Chief Maskepetoon (The Broken Arm), was talking to him.

Big Bear had met those "fathers," but he could think of no use for what they said or for the holy water they carried. The gifts of the Bear Spirit and of The Only Great Spirit, who had given his People the whole Earth and everything good for life with it—that was more than enough for him. As was the ecstatic, dangerous joy of Blackfoot raids: stealthy approach, retreat, silent stalk and circle, counter-raid, attack, and night herds of horses galloping.

One spring young Big Bear with his companions ran west to haunt Blackfoot camps all summer. They captured scores of horses, and Big Bear sent all his horses back to Black Powder while staying on the prairie till autumn, living a season of daring, pursuit, and raid. When the youths returned at last, all alive and with still more horses, Big Bear told a story during his honour dance that is still recounted in the Cree oral tradition. His greatest summer adventure was not horse stealing: it was a dream. A Spirit guided him to a vision of horses in a huge cave. They were his, hundreds of them; he could just walk into the herd and take the one at the centre. So he walked forward, but a giant stallion reared his black hoofs beating over him, and he stooped to protect himself. Instantly the horses vanished. Too bad you stooped, said the Spirit. Now you'll never be rich in horses.

Therefore, to fulfill the stooping vision, Big Bear gave away every horse he had taken that summer, keeping only one because no one would accept the last. His People celebrated him even louder with songs and dancing until Big Bear laughed with them, shouting, Now I feel very handsome! And the band rejoiced; they had a fine chief, who had a brave and generous son who received powerful guidance from visions but nevertheless could still laugh at his scarred appearance. A Young Man to be cherished, his stories to be remembered.

Good years of growing into complete manhood followed. Sometimes, alone on the evening prairie, Big Bear heard the grass tear between his horse's teeth, sensed the gentle burble of its stomach, and a sadness would come over him. His world was changing. The Elders said, Something is wrong with the buffalo. Their raids on the Blackfoot were becoming less about the prestige of horse stealing and much more about having enough buffalo to eat. The once-great herds seemed to be shrinking farther south, and to find them, the Cree had to push farther into the lands of the Blackfoot, who in turn pushed harder against the Crow, the Shoshone, the Cheyenne. How would it continue if, as they heard, more Whites than ever were rushing in beyond the border, not only by cart and boat, but on iron rails laid down for a smoke-blasting machine that dragged wagons full of them faster than a horse could gallop. How, under the Creator, would the world go on?

Big Bear's vision on Bull's Forehead Hill took place deep in Blackfoot territory, and its fulfillment gave him particular power against them. To live, both Plains Cree and Blackfoot bands needed horses and buffalo, but they also needed to capture women. There were never enough mature women for the endless labour of a hunting camp: bearing and caring for children, digging roots and gathering berries and continually cooking, skinning and stretching furs, skinning and butchering buffalo before they spoiled in the heat, cutting meat into strips to dry in the sun and pounding it into powder for pemmican, scraping and tanning hides, sewing clothing, packing and carrying the camp by backpack and dog- and horse-travois to follow the herds while the armed men walked wide as guards or rode ahead scouting for animals or enemies, one or the other—who could say what might appear over the next horizon? Only strong women made prairie hunting life possible, and that meant endless raids to capture them from your enemies.

Though Black Powder's band still wintered between The Little Hills and Jackfish Lake, the fur animals there were largely gone. The band's main trade with the Company was no longer in spring with furs at Carlton, but rather in autumn at Fort Pitt with buffalo hides and pemmican. The Company needed prairie pemmican to feed their voyageurs rowing or tracking their huge York boats, filled with trade goods from Hudson Bay and fur from farther north, where there were still fur animals.

In the fall when Big Bear turned twenty-two, a Blackfoot war party destroyed a Cree camp within sight of Fort Pitt. Chief Man Who Makes the War Whoop survived, and that winter he travelled among bands, persuading them to give him their pledge for a revenge attack when the grass was green enough for horses. Among ten other chiefs, Black Powder pledged his band's pipe, their sacred commitment to honour and honesty. The artist Paul Kane, travelling among Company posts (1848), drew pictures of both Cree chiefs, which, they thought, would give them special war power. But, unknown to them, the Blackfoot were planning an even larger expedition, and before the Cree could finish their Thirst Dance in preparation, more than five hundred Blackfoot warriors had advanced again toward Fort Pitt. Scouts encountered scouts, the Blackfoot attacked, and though the Cree killed ten attackers and drove them off, eighteen of their huge gathering were killed and forty wounded. Big Bear fought hard; his Bear

medicine protected him, and he was not wounded, but in this series of attacks the Blackfoot obviously had stronger medicine than the Plains Cree. The Spirits had told them clearly—who could understand why?—that now was no time for revenge.

Big Bear had proven himself an outstanding hunter and warrior, a generous man who received deep spiritual vision. He was too young to be a band councillor, but he was recognized as a Worthy Young Man who, because of his hunting and war exploits, soon sat in the Warrior Society circle and took part in their ceremonial dances. One day (1847–48) the father of a Cree-Saulteaux girl named Sayos came to Black Powder's lodge leading two fine horses. Several days later a lodge of new hides stood beside the chief's lodge, and when Big Bear entered, Sayos greeted him with a pair of new moccasins that fit him exactly. The families exchanged other gifts, clothing, and horses, and Sayos and Big Bear became wife and husband. He would eventually have five wives: the hospitality and generosity expected of a Cree leader demanded more work than any one or two women could provide, but Sayos would remain his lifelong love and bear him the most children.

Their first baby was a girl they named Nowakich, their second a son, Twin Wolverine, a name from their Saulteaux boreal past. While they wintered in The Little Hills in 1851,

Sayos bore a second son, whom they named Imasees, which translates as Little Wild Man or Little Bad Man. This little man would grow into the stocky, powerful image of his father but with an intense, chiselled face and downturned lips that rarely laughed. No one could know how profoundly that wild or bad would reveal itself.

(In 1989, Imasees's mother will be called Na-tachi-skau-n, or simply Joanne in sworn statements deposited at the American Museum of Natural History in New York. The same statements will name Imasees as Little Bear.)

The seasonal cycles of band hunting continued in the 1850s. Not raids, but providing food and protection for his band and growing family, were Big Bear's daily life. The Cree had established their buffalo territory on the plains, and though there were still clashes with the Blackfoot Confederacy, a mutual need for less violence had Elders in both tribes advocating peace. One Cree in particular, Chief Maskepetoon—who had allowed himself to be touched by Methodist Rundle's holy water and, it was said, could hear Christian Cree words on birch bark or paper—gradually became a powerful peace negotiator.

Years before, while the chief was away raiding, Blackfoot warriors had destroyed his camp, killing his aged father. Maskepetoon was told the name of his father's killer, but instead of pursuing revenge, he led his People into the Beaver Hills for healing. He began to talk aloud about the wisdom of peace. Now, it was told, Cree warriors had brought several Blackfoot into Maskepetoon's camp and called out the name of the killer. The Blackfoot men were surrounded; the killer stood motionless facing the chief, waiting like a warrior for whatever would hit him.

Maskepetoon turned, went into his lodge, and emerged with his ceremonial warrior clothes, the suit of beads and quills and scalps he had not worn for years. Put this on, he said in Blackfoot, and after the man had done that he told him to mount the horse tied beside his lodge. Then Maskepetoon looked directly at him.

Both my hands are empty, he said. You took my father from me, so now I ask you to be my father. Wear my clothes, ride my horse, and when your People ask you how it is you are still alive, tell them it is because Maskepetoon has taken his revenge.

The Blackfoot warrior slid off the horse; he took Maskepetoon in his arms and held him hard against his heart.

My son, he said. You have killed me.

As this story was carried across the plains and along the rivers of the boreal forest by both the People and White missionaries, the Cree and Blackfoot Elders had a powerful teaching for their Young Men. Perhaps there were greater, braver honours to be attained than stealing and bloody coups and killing. Consider the profound pre-eminence of magnanimity and hospitality, the hard discipline of forgiveness. Who showed the greater courage: a warrior who fought wars with enemies or a man who rode unarmed into an enemy camp and tried to talk peace? Slowly, peace treaties—the Cree called them *âsotamâkêwin*, meaning "promise"—among the tribes reached over the prairie, lasting almost four years.

Big Bear had given up the canoe of his boreal ancestors and become a superb horseman. The Hudson's Bay Company now brought goods up the North Saskatchewan to Carlton and Pitt and Edmonton and Rocky Mountain House in huge York boats dragged by men with ropes over their shoulders, but Big Bear remembered the Company governor, George Simpson, crowned by a black beaver hat and sitting stiff like a grand chief in his canoe while his voyageurs paddled him past so swiftly that the evening sun rippled the river into floating fire. He never met "Little Emperor" Simpson, not even at Pitt, where he now traded most often.

Then one spring (1861), after a Cree war party had ruined the always precarious peace promises by killing a Blackfoot chief and the tribe had retaliated by killing twenty Cree camped near Fort Pitt, the chief factor there told Big Bear something very strange.

The factor's name was James Simpson. Big Bear had known him for fifteen years as a trader, always fair with his weights and counting. Now, drinking tea with him in his log house inside the high spruce palisades of the trading post, Simpson told him that his mother had been a Cree-Scots woman and his father the Little Emperor.

James Simpson said, I was his first son. I heard he died last fall (September 1860), in the far east, Montreal.

First son. After a moment Big Bear asked, What is that, Montreal?

A place where many Whites live close together. Sixty thousand, more people than there are on the prairie, or were, even before the smallpox.

More Whites than Red River?

Twenty times. I went to school there. They have houses six floors high on an island where their river is three times wider than our Saskatchewan. Ships come from across oceans, from everywhere in the world. They have a railroad too, though not as long as the Americans'. My father told me they were talking about it.

About what?

Building a railroad to Red River. My father didn't like that, he said too many Whites would come and ruin the Company trade. But he's gone, so they must be thinking about it again. Maybe a railroad over the prairie.

Could that be believed? Simpson sat on his thick buffalo robe as lightly as a Cree, but it was spread on a wooden floor, not good earth. His face slanted into a straggly brown beard—he looked so White, but spoke the language clear as any Elder.

And Big Bear remembered a disturbing boyhood dream of uncountable Whites streaming from somewhere east and south onto the prairie and chopping down trees and pounding together square houses in every river valley, so many houses that there was no wood to shelter People from winter storms. The Elders had marvelled when he told them. Look at the Whites here, they advised him. We've known them from Elders beyond Elders, and the places they build with posts are no more than specks four days apart along one river. What can your dream mean?

Catherine, Simpson's wife, joined them with a kettle of steaming water for the pot. A beautiful woman, Big Bear thought, with her eyes shining black against her dark skin. How could she be Gabriel Dumont's, the ugly Métis leader's, sister?—and he had to laugh at himself. Simpson looked up, and Big Bear could only offer him tobacco for his pipe, though Simpson had bales of it and he had no more than what filled his pouch. Simpson cut off a plug, and Big Bear could ask:

His first son. So, are you, now, the Company's Big Boss?

Simpson watched the smoke curl until he passed the short pipe to Catherine. I have my father's blood, he said, and name. He paid for my school as long as I could stand it … I saw him five times in my life … no … no, he had enough children, especially all White ones. I'll never have more from him.

What more would you need? You'll grow rich trading with me.

They laughed together, seated on the robe drinking tea and smoking. As they did every fall at Fort Pitt, and sometimes in summer when Simpson brought his well-bred horses to the Cree on the plains. A good horse could cost four bags of pemmican, but they were needed more than ever because, with renewed enemy attacks, there were not enough Young Men left to steal them from the Blackfoot or Shoshone even when they pushed that far south. And sometimes now whole camps of Blackfoot were naked beggars, on foot because they had given away their horses and everything else for the whisky that Whites carted from the Missouri. Some warriors went crazy drinking it, and often the women and Elders couldn't stop them.

Simpson told Big Bear, Those bastards are American. They're not supposed to drag their rotgut over the border. But there's no Canadian here to stop them.

Big Bear snorted. That Medicine Line is for Whites. The land is ours; the Blackfoot have to protect it themselves.

But you know whisky, Simpson said. You've drunk it.

Enough to feel sick, not become stupid.

Once that summer (1861), when Black Powder's band was hunting with their Assiniboine allies so far south that the Sweetgrass Hills in Montana loomed over the horizon, they heard the shriek of carts from beyond the folds of long land. Several Assiniboine whooped Whisky! so loud that their horses leaped, but next morning the Cree left them to retreat north. As bad as whisky men were with their wooden barrels and stinking liquor pails and dippers, they always held a short gun in one hand while pouring, guns that fired six bullets as fast as they could pull the trigger.

For seasons on end Maskepetoon and his two sons rode to the Blood and Peigan, who were often more open to talk than the Siksika, trying to renegotiate peace treaties with the Blackfoot. He argued, We all want to live, and we all need buffalo. Honour the Creator with prayers, with the pipe and songs, and honour the promises between us in the hard life we all live. He carried a Bible with him now; he read it aloud in Cree and then translated the words into Blackfoot. He told them: This holy book tells of a Prince of Peace who would save all Peoples from evil. Listen to the Prince of Peace!

But there were always enough Young Men mourning their brothers, both Blackfoot and Cree, who could not endure such words. They would leave Maskepetoon and the Elders to their talk and ride away, ashamed that they had not protected their dead or wounded comrades and dreaming not of peace but of bloody revenge.

Into these years of the Buffalo Wars came pestilence. Scarlet fever attacked the Blackfoot, and during the winter of 1864–65 more than a thousand died. That same fall the supply brigade from Hudson Bay brought measles to Edmonton, and both Métis and Cree died, including many of Maskepetoon's and Sweetgrass's People. That did not stop the inter-tribal violence. Big Bear was trading in Pitt when Blackfoot laid siege to the tiny post on the flats beside the North Saskatchewan; they had a few rifles, bows, and knives, but they galloped around the palisade screaming war cries and taunting the Cree to come out and fight. Simpson had left the Company to breed horses near Red River, and the new factor offered Big Bear and his men Company horses to ride out and drive them off. But Big Bear refused. Let them scream, he said, they'll soon get tired. And finally the Blackfoot did leave, with nothing.

In the winter of 1864–65, Black Powder's crier walked through the camp in The Little Hills shouting a sad message. The chief was dead. His body lay in his lodge but his soul was gone, his neck cold as ice.

In deep mourning, the band began their death ceremonies, so that Black Powder's soul would not need to wander long to reach the land of the dead. In life or death the band was one; communal song and sorrow and happiness and prayer held their world together. They dressed the body in ceremonial clothes, they recounted Black Powder's war record and his long, wise leadership, they gathered around his body to weep. The family unbound their hair; several gashed their arms and legs until their bare bodies wept blood. Then four aged warriors lifted the corpse on a buffalo hide and, followed by the wailing band, carried it to the platform prepared between the forks of aspen. Big Bear sang the death song over the cries of mourning while the men wrapped the body in rawhide and bound it tight. Then they walked away between the pale trees, still weeping.

After four days they gathered to the crier's call for prayers, the pipe ceremony, the ritual opening of the chief's bundle, and a final honour feast of buffalo meat and dried saskatoon soup.

The Plains Cree band of some hundred People now needed a chief. Black Powder's oldest son, Big Bear, was forty years old. All his life he had observed how a chief unites a band, even though anyone is free to leave at any time and join another band. A chief led by communal agreement, not by orders; People respected him for being wise and generous with gifts and hospitality, they followed him because he fought and hunted and cared for every person in his band. Above all else, a chief was a man who served others.

The band respected Big Bear because he was an even-tempered, thoughtful man who played with children and laughed at himself, who dreamed dreams and received visions, a person whom smallpox could not kill, but even more because his spirit helper was the Great Parent of Bear, who had given him a powerful bundle that protected him from every harm during years of defending his People. His honour stories had been sung at Thirst Dance ceremonies, from his greatest warrior deeds of dodging through enemy arrows or bullets to club a warrior and take his scalp, to facing an enemy with only a war club or a knife, or stealing into a Blackfoot camp and galloping away with the buffalo runner tied beside the lodge of a war chief. And how, when bloody violence between Cree and Blackfoot continued endlessly, one winter he had carried his band's medicine pipe bundle through the snow to eight Plains Cree chiefs and persuaded them to pledge their peace on the pipe. Then in spring he rode to Blackfoot camps with the pipe and convinced them to come together to make peace with the Cree. Like the venerable Maskepetoon, he was a devastating warrior who also had the courage to stop killing.

There was consensus: Big Bear should follow in his father's footsteps. He was a mature family man, with a daughter old enough for marriage and two sons already riding with the Young Men to hunt or watch for enemies. And he accepted the band's communal call to duty. He had no illusions of power; he knew he needed more guidance, so he allied himself with Sweetgrass, the elder statesman among the Plains Cree trading at Fort Pitt. But as they had all feared, the tribal wars over buffalo grew steadily worse.

About the time that Big Bear was chosen chief, far away in the east the Charlottetown and Quebec conferences were beginning to shape the colonial provinces of British

North America into the nation of Canada. Big Bear could not know that John A. Macdonald, one of the leaders of that Confederation movement, would soon become the most powerful person in deciding the destiny of all prairie People.

The summer after Big Bear became a chief, the northern prairie tribes faced something more ominous than distant White politics or the wars and hunger and disease they continually struggled with. That summer they found that the Iron Stone was gone.

Reverend Robert Rundle, who listed 592 Cree in his Baptism Book by the Christian names he gave them, left Edmonton in 1848, and a new Methodist missionary came from Upper Canada (Ontario) to build a log church on the North Saskatchewan River halfway between Fort Pitt and Edmonton. He called the place Victoria after the Great Mother he was always talking about. This George McDougall with his son John ripped up large plots of earth for potatoes—very good food, bigger and sweeter than wild turnips—and every spring they hunted buffalo on the prairie with Cree bands led by Chiefs Maskepetoon and Pakan. They were powerful God-men both in talking and acting; it was said they intended to build another church on the Bow River, where even the Company had never had a trading post for more than a year before the Blackfoot burned it down. In 1869, George McDougall wrote to his mission director in Toronto:

> "August 23, Iron Creek: This beautiful stream derives its name from a strange formation said to be pure iron. The piece weighs 300 pounds.... Tradition says that it has lain out on the hill ever since the place was first visited by Na-ne-boo-sho after the flood had retired. For ages the tribes of the Blackfoot and Cree have gathered their clans to pay homage to this wonderful manitoo. Three years ago [1866] one of our people put the idol in his cart and brought it to [our settlement] Victoria."

In July 1874, he mentioned the stone again (apparently it had gained weight):

> "I have sent on to Red River a meteoric stone weighing 400 pounds, the great memento of the plains, and requested Brother Young to forward it to your address. I intended it for Victoria College [Cobourg, Ontario]...."

Since before time, the sacred Iron Stone had rested on its solitary, pointed hill near the Battle River, overlooking the long ravines of Iron Creek. From beside it the Plains People could see the complete circle of Earth, could look west and north and east to the endless forests, and south over the scattered coppice of aspen fading into the light of the prairie where they found their daily food. The Blackfoot had dedicated the stone to Old Man Buffalo, guardian spirit of buffalo and protector of everyone who came to pray, and when the Cree moved onto the plains, they too worshipped there, chanting prayers and songs, leaving thank offerings for the gifts given, for the continuing hope of life for themselves and their children.

Now the Iron Stone was gone. Sweetgrass said bitterly, It's lying beside McDougall's church in Victoria. Our Father Lacombe would never have done that.

Big Bear answered nothing. He loved the older chief as he had loved his father, but he was concerned that Sweetgrass had let Lacombe baptize him. Big Bear could not quite trust any God-man. Until now they had done no real harm and were friendly enough to People, but they were always arguing with one another about an incomprehensible White "God" who was forever enraged about something. Big Bear had no feeling, no intuition, no dream that he should listen to any of them. And this inexplicable theft confirmed his refusal. Here was more proof that Whites respected only their own ways of honouring the Creator: the Methodists, who had baptized Maskepetoon and continued to help him promote peace, seemingly felt no shame in stealing the Stone.

People were stunned by the theft, and the Elders foresaw certain disaster. Disease, starvation, more bitter war must follow such a desecration. Cree Chief Pakan, whose band grew acres of Methodist potatoes east of Victoria, had nothing to say; his People could not live without buffalo either. And for several years the buffalo did continue to come north, though sometimes the tribes were forced to hunt so closely together that several men might be wounded or even killed before the chiefs could negotiate a mutual withdrawal. All the beautiful Young Men, so quick to be shamed and hot-blooded on their swift horses and longing for vengeance, were always so hard to hold in check.

And more stories arrived from the east. It was said that four or five White tribes had made a treaty and now had one Big Chief and one giant country called Canada. Big Bear rolled the word around in his mouth. In Cree it echoed the word *kanâta*, meaning "the place that is clean," though he doubted it was. The chief's name, Macdonald, sounded Methodist.

In 1870, smallpox found the Cree again. The previous fall Blackfoot had unwittingly stolen infected blankets from a Missouri riverboat, and throughout the winter the disease spread terror among them. As soon as he heard, Big Bear moved farther north, his band scattering beyond the North Saskatchewan, and so James Simpson with his horses to trade did not find him until late summer.

The Elders foretold this, Big Bear said sadly. Four years after Methodists stole Old Man Buffalo, we have smallpox.

Simpson said, Maybe it won't attack your band if you stay north of the river.

Maybe we can stay long enough—if your good horses help us fish.

That evening they drank tea and smoked and remembered Chief Maskepetoon, who that spring had again ridden to the Blackfoot to make peace. In the camp of his Blackfoot father he had been greeted with ceremony and joy. But before they could talk, a Blackfoot named Big Swan, who had fought with Cree near Edmonton just days before, fired a shot and knocked the old man from his horse. In a frenzy of hatred, over the shouts of consternation and grief from the Elders, the warriors dragged Maskepetoon's body out onto the prairie, hacked it up, and left the pieces to the dogs.

Big Bear said, He was our peace chief. There can only be more war.

Simpson murmured, Perhaps war with the Whites too.

Big Bear looked up. Why would we fight Whites?

Red River, Simpson said. Just this spring Canada marched in a thousand soldiers and chased Louis Riel across the border into the States. Half those soldiers are still there.

The Métis know what wars they want to fight. We are People.

Haven't you heard? The Métis made Riel chief of Red River because they heard the Hudson's Bay Company had sold the land to Canada.

Sold? What land?

Simpson said, All the land, everything around Red River, and even here where you live.

The Company has no land, just the spots where People once agreed they could build posts to trade with us.

They say Canada bought the whole land from them, everything north of the border to the mountains.

After a long pause of incomprehension, Big Bear asked, Did your father say that? That the Company *owns* our land?

Simpson snorted. Huh! My father thought he owned everything he stepped on. He doesn't matter, but Macdonald in Ottawa matters. He says he's bought all the land.

How can anyone "buy" or "own" land?

The question Big Bear would ask many times in the coming years. And no one would give him any more comfort than James Simpson:

I think maybe Whites can do more than we can dream of.

The trader was surprised at how many horses Big Bear's band bartered for despite its poverty. The chief did not tell him that they were planning war. Their Assiniboine allies had begun it by sending a tobacco message: The Blackfoot are ravaged by smallpox; come, now is the time to destroy them. We will avenge your peace chief Maskepetoon, and we will have the prairie and buffalo to ourselves.

More than twenty Cree bands, including those of Big Bear and his close friend Little Pine, smoked the tobacco, and though Sweetgrass was too old for battle, most of his Young Men came as well. In early October 1870, the Cree met the Assiniboine in the Vermillion Hills and more than six hundred warriors rode west together, the largest force they had ever assembled.

They finally reached the Little Bow River and sent out scouts. They readied their Bay muzzle-loaders and rifles, their bows and arrows, spears, war clubs, and knives, but one day in council, Assiniboine Chief Piapot told them he had dreamed a dream. He had seen a buffalo with iron horns charging through camp, goring, tossing warriors aside in bloody pieces; clearly, his guardian spirit was warning him not to commit war. But the other leaders did not agree: they were eight days into Blackfoot territory and still had not met one single enemy! So next day, while Piapot and some followers turned back, almost six hundred warriors continued south to the Oldman River, where the scouts had discovered a Blood camp within sight of the mountains. They attacked before dawn.

But, unknown to them, several much larger bands of Peigan and Blood were camped nearby, and before the Cree and Assiniboine could completely destroy the smaller camp, they were in turn attacked. These Blackfoot were armed with the latest Winchester repeater rifles and Colt revolvers traded from the Americans, and they drove the invaders back over the open prairie and into the Oldman River coulees where a few years later Whites would dig the coal mines of Lethbridge. There, after four more hours of ferocious fighting, forty Blackfoot were killed and fifty wounded, while the Cree allies escaped total annihilation only by leaving three hundred of their dead on the cliffs and in the coulees and river valley when they retreated. They were so outgunned that Jerry Potts, a half-Blood warrior who later became a guide for the North West Mounted Police, said, "You could shut your eyes and still be sure to kill a Cree." The Blackfoot named that place Assini-etomochi, Where They Slaughtered the Cree.

CHAPTER FOUR

Come, Talk to Us

Chief's Son's Hand protected Big Bear in the disastrous battle on the Oldman River; he wore the paw around his neck and was unharmed. His sons Twin Wolverine and Imasees also returned home not badly wounded. But the bodies of so many warriors from so many bands were left behind to be shamefully mutilated by the enemy that Cree mourning continued all winter. And in the nights when Big Bear lay sleepless under his buffalo robes, he slowly came to realize that the unbelievable stories they had heard about the Americans fighting among themselves—how in their battles uncountable thousands of men were destroyed in a single day, and almost as many horses—were true. Such White wars actually happened. The Blood and Peigan had shown them how American guns could kill.

Through the winter nights, with all his relations breathing around him, Big Bear remembered again and again riding south in darkness with the crunch of frosted grass under his horse's hooves, and then, along the crest of the plain, the jagged wall of snow-covered mountains slowly rising into light before him. The Cree warriors charged screaming with him into the Blood camp, the lodge-hide split at the stab of his knife, a child's eyes stared up at him—and then the sudden, terrifying revelation of blazing mountains, like a stampede of white buffalo charging up over him, trampling all the Cree among the Blood lodges. He had thought it had been revealed only to Piapot, but gradually he knew he had to think differently. He began to understand something he could never have comprehended without that little child's eyes and the mountains of white buffalo vision when they attacked the Blood and had been attacked in turn by repeater rifles and revolvers, beaten back into the coulees, retreat upon desperate retreat, until they fell from the cliffs into the Oldman River. He finally understood what he should have recognized in the dawn light: that the honourable battles of hand-to-hand combat with an enemy you knew by name were gone. Brutal, faceless killing war had come, war fought at such long range you could barely see a body nor find a breath between the unending bullets. Never on Earth would there be enough People to survive such capability for slaughter.

So, think different. For People to live, they must try to think like Whites too.

That winter, Sweetgrass, Big Bear, Little Pine, and all the chiefs along the river from Carlton to Rocky Mountain House agreed: war among the Plains People must end. Sweetgrass negotiated a peace treaty with the Blackfoot so that the Cree could safely visit Chief Factor William Christie of the Hudson's Bay Company at Edmonton. On April 13, 1871, Christie sent a long letter to Lieutenant-Governor Archibald at Red River that declared: "The buffalo will soon be exterminated.... The establishment of law and order in the Saskatchewan District is of most vital importance to the interest of Canada...." And to his letter he attached messages from the Cree:

> "The Chief Sweet Grass, the Chief of the country:
>
> "Great Father—I shake hands with you, and bid you welcome. We heard our lands were sold and we did not like it; we don't want to sell our lands; it is our property, and no one has a right to sell them.
>
> "Our country is getting ruined of fur-bearing animals, hitherto our sole support, and now we are poor and want help—we want you to pity us. We want cattle, tools, agricultural implements, and assistance in everything when we come to settle— our country is no longer able to support us.

"Make provision for us against years of starvation. We have had great starvation the past winter, the small-pox took away many of our people, the old, young, and children.

"We want you to stop the Americans from coming to trade on our lands, and giving firewater, ammunition and arms to our enemies, the Blackfeet.

"We made a peace this winter with the Blackfeet. Our young men are foolish, it may not last long.

"We invite you to come and see us and speak with us. If you can't come yourself, send some one in your place.

"We send these words by our Master, Mr. Christie, in whom we have every confidence. That is all."

Several other chiefs added their words, but Big Bear did not. James Simpson had told him that the English translation of Cree was always a bit slanted, huh! it was hard enough to know what writing meant even if you knew English! Big Bear thought that Sweetgrass—Lacombe had baptized him Abraham—went too far into Company talk about trade, too much into missionary talk about settlement, about pity. Only the Great Spirit's pity meant anything. But he agreed with the statement about land. The Big Whites must come and explain what "sell land," "Governor," and "Great Mother" meant. And where was Canada in this letter? Big Boss Macdonald?

But despite this letter, and despite the arrival of a young soldier named William Butler who said he was travelling the North-West on orders by Prime Minister Macdonald and would give their messages directly to him, no one of authority came to talk. The Cree did hear that the forest Saulteaux and Woods Cree from Red River to Lake of the Woods were talking with Canada about a treaty for land to build a road; but they could not agree because the chiefs declared, "All this is our property where you have come. The Great Spirit planted us on this ground." The talking would continue for another two years.

Nevertheless, talking was good; you saw Whites face to face, you knew where they were and what they were doing, they had to answer you. Not like the disaster on the Oldman River, where the Cree had not known about Fort Whoop-Up, or about trade in repeater rifles and bullets, or about the Major Baker massacre of 170 Peigan men, women, and children by the United States Army that had driven the remaining Peigan north, so that they were on the Oldman River and could defend their Blood allies.

For four years Big Bear listened while his band hunted the plains and the winter boreal forest. They avoided Whites except for essential trade at Fort Pitt. Three wives now lived in his lodge, and the second had borne another son, Kingbird. Imasees had become a formidable Young Man, and Nowakich and Twin Wolverine were married. Nowakich's husband was Lone Man, a fine warrior and perceptive thinker, the son of a Blackfoot woman captured in a raid; he became Big Bear's closest confidant. Big Bear's independent leadership attracted more and more Cree to his band, but now the northern buffalo grazed in small, scattered herds and, despite widespread peace with the Blackfoot, were increasingly difficult to find. Starvation threatened.

Many Métis had left Red River after 1870 when Canadian militia chased Louis Riel into the United States. They settled along the South Saskatchewan River near Batoche. But soon the buffalo no longer grazed there, and they were forced to hunt the same herds as the Cree and Blackfoot much farther south. The Métis summer hunts were massively organized, with a hunt captain and companies of ten policing every aspect of camp life to ensure every possible animal was taken. The captain of the 1873 hunt was

Gabriel Dumont, an extraordinary marksman of enormous prestige and ego. On the plains, Big Bear discovered that his Cree and the Métis had found the same scattering of buffalo, and he rode into Dumont's camp to negotiate an equitable hunting arrangement. But the captain bellowed, No! The whole herd belonged to them. Big Bear walked out of Dumont's lodge and later sent six Young Men to haze part of the herd over the river so that the Cree could hunt them undisturbed by the Métis.

But Dumont and his scouts discovered the tactic and galloped to confront Big Bear. He denied nothing. His People needed food too; they could share what the Creator had given. At that, Dumont lashed out:

"You're a dirty, thieving chief … and if any of your Young Men have had a hand in this, it won't be well for you."

Insulted before his People, Big Bear walked away. As punishment, the Métis soldiers seized a Cree cart and gave it to one of their hunters. Big Bear would not acknowledge that the Métis had any more claim to the buffalo than he did, nor was he so stupid as to fight. His band broke camp to hunt elsewhere.

But no Cree forgot that confrontation or Big Bear's unshaken dignity at public humiliation. Years later John Kerr, an Ontario adventurer who lived with the Métis, told the story. By then Big Bear was a North-West Rebellion villain though he had shot no one, and Gabriel Dumont a hero despite the fact that at Fish Creek he had killed twelve Canadians with his unerring rifle.

Big Bear's band tried to avoid Americans who spread like smallpox across the border as much as they tried to avoid the Métis. Not only did the Americans build fortified posts such as Whoop-Up, Standoff, and Kipp in Blackfoot territory to lure People into trade for whisky, but the ox trains of wolfers loaded with poison for wolves and barrels of rotgut followed them everywhere. No sooner was a buffalo skinned than the hide was traded for stupefied drunkenness and the carcass poisoned to kill wolves for their fur.

Canada claimed all territory north of the Medicine Line, but its government had no way of stopping Americans from crossing the border and doing whatever they pleased. The Americans hauled hides, however they acquired them, back to Fort Benton and shipped them down the Missouri to be made into belts in their eastern factories. The Hudson's Bay Company petitioned Ottawa again and again, reporting their trade ruined by illegal businesses that destroyed the Plains People, but nothing happened. Until May 1873, when six American whisky louts in the Cypress Hills massacred forty drunken Assiniboine and violated both women and children. Only then did Macdonald legislate the North West Mounted Police into existence, to enforce Canadian law on the prairies. A hundred and fifty men arrived in Red River from Canada that summer.

The Plains Cree heard this, heard how more men were being recruited and trained all winter. In July 1874, four hundred police, with hundreds of horses and workers and supply carts, started their monumental trek west for the Cypress Hills and Fort Whoop-Up. About the same time, Big Bear learned that George McDougall in Victoria had had the Iron Stone heaved into a cart and sent shrieking off to Red River.

(For well over a century, Old Man Buffalo survived in Ontario, but in 2008 he is on display in the Syncrude Gallery of Aboriginal Culture at the Royal Alberta Museum in Edmonton. As you approach, the gleaming black, pock-marked shape shifts into a conical human head; a great eagle-beaked nose with deep nostrils and mouth emerge. After a moment you recognize that the civilized steel that holds the head on its stand is clamped precisely through that open mouth, so it cannot utter a sound.)

So, while Old Man Buffalo was being dragged east, an army of Whites was marching west: was this the new order of protection under which People must now somehow live?

Big Bear contemplated the smoke drifting from his pipe. Then he stood up, walked between the lodges and evening fires and women and men and dogs and children chasing one another for happiness—there were more than five hundred in his band now, because Lucky Man and his followers had just come—and went onto the silent prairie, where prayer was possible. And, perhaps, if the Spirits were compassionate, vision. He remembered the McDougall log church, and how the Iron Stone had been fixed in humiliation beside it for twice four years. He could not count the times he had brought thank offerings when the Stone rested on the hill, where the dust of buffalo lay beyond every horizon.

Did the Spirits have no power once the Stone was torn from its sacred hilltop? Fenced into that little churchyard in the valley, forced to hear those Christian songs? How could Chief Pakan and his band walk past into that square building when they, too, had once left offerings on the hill? It must be the land; even Old Man Buffalo had no power without it.

And yet ... despite the violation, Big Bear felt a certain respect for McDougall father and son. Sometimes he felt he could forgive them because they were so generous, their word so trustworthy. One autumn, when Big Bear's band was starving, they dug up acres of Methodist potatoes, and the McDougalls, when they found out, just said, Fine, you needed food. They suffered too when buffalo couldn't be found, but also from the silent enemy smallpox: John's wife and two children were in the Victoria cemetery with many Cree. But strangely, Maskepetoon had been more committed to peace than these contradictory Whites; their God seemed very violent at times, and, they preached, Only we know how to deal with Him, so listen to us!

The immense land remained. Big Bear stood, listening. No one could drag it away in a cart. The land grew grass, grass fed buffalo, buffalo fed People. They were all land. They would remain; he prayed.

The North West Mounted Police hauled themselves west over the prairie along the Medicine Line border. At La Roche Percée, one column rode north for Edmonton via Carlton while the other continued west. Big Bear's band heard of both columns' slow progress throughout the summer. The cart treks the Métis and traders and missionaries made routinely every year became overwhelming sagas of drought and mud and dying horses for these Whites who were supposed to guard the country for Canada. The western contingent got lost between the Bow and Oldman rivers; they could not find Fort Whoop-Up to arrest the illegal Americans there, though they searched for two weeks. Finally, worn and starving, they trekked south into Montana, where they met the half-Blood

Jerry Potts in Fort Benton, who led them back into Canada on the wide Whoop-Up wagon trail two hundred and thirty miles to the fort. They found neither trader nor whisky inside its palisade, only one crippled White man and four Blood women. No shot was fired nor voice raised. The women cooked the exhausted Canadians all the buffalo they could eat.

While the Mounted Police were getting lost, Company trader William McKay visited the Cree on the plains in the name, he said, of the Great Mother. He explained that the police would "mark out the line between Her territories and those of the United States so that Her Indian and White subjects might know where the lands of the Queen begin." The police had no military purpose but had come to "preserve the Queen's law and order," especially now that crews were surveying routes for railroad and telegraph lines to be built across the prairie. Big Bear and his council were disturbed. The Queen's land? The Queen's law? A railroad? McKay could only repeat the words he had been told— someone else would come to explain more—then he gave them tea, sugar, tobacco, and, oddly, fifteen scalping knives and left for the next band.

During the summer of 1874, the Plains Cree began to comprehend what a mass of Whites was pouring in upon them. Police troops, surveyors for railroad and telegraph lines, land speculators, settlers trekking their carts along the Carlton Trail from Red River to Pitt and Victoria and Edmonton. The first sternwheeler steamer on the Saskatchewan River crawled over shoals and rapids from Lake Winnipeg to Carlton filled with passengers and three hundred cartloads of Company freight.

And, after two years of talk, the Lake of the Woods–Red River People settled with the government commissioners on agreements they called Treaty One and Treaty Two. In 1874, new commissioners then called the central Qu'Appelle Cree and Assiniboine People together to enact a similar treaty for their prairie lands. Big Bear heard how the Saulteaux speaker Gambler had tried to negotiate a list of conditions with Lieutenant-Governor Alexander Morris, arguing, "The Company has stolen our land.... The earth, trees, grass, stones, everything I see with my eyes." The Cree speaker Pis-qua pointed at Company Factor McDonald and declared, "You told me you had sold your land for 300,000 pounds. We want that money." But the talking went nowhere; Morris stubbornly repeated he had no authority to make major changes for them to the treaty already negotiated at Lake of the Woods, and after barely six days of meetings that would determine their lives forever, the Qu'Appelle chiefs signed Treaty Four. An excellent treaty, Morris said in congratulation, which gave them "the full breadth and width of the Queen's goodness"—five dollars per person per year forever.

It was now four years after Sweetgrass's Edmonton letter, and still no commissioner had come to talk with the North Saskatchewan Plains Cree. Then, during the summer of 1875, after the SS *Northcote* had burned its way two thousand river miles from Lake Winnipeg to Edmonton and back, three Cree warriors stopped a telegraph crew hanging their endless wire in the air approaching Pitt. The leader spoke for Mista-wasis (Big Child), head of the Carlton People, who declared that the crew would not cut down one more Cree tree to hang up its wire, which would certainly frighten their animals away, until a treaty was made. The contractor "could do nothing but put all the wire, insulators, brackets, etc., in one large pile" and return to Carlton. Lieutenant-Governor Morris at Red River heard his report that same day, by telegraph, and within two weeks a messenger was driving to visit every Cree band in the Saskatchewan district and the plains. The government messenger was missionary George McDougall, who had stolen Old Man Buffalo and shipped him away.

Considering McDougall's hairy face—not smooth like the Catholic Lacombe's—Big Bear tried to remember why he respected him. McDougall sat in the band's place of honour, on the chief's left in the council circle, with his wagonload of presents piled behind him, and spoke about the Queen who loved all her children so much, her Red as much as her White. Thousands of her Red children had already taken her hand, through her commissioners, in five great treaties, and next summer the same commissioners would come and make treaty with them too. Big Bear was thinking, If the Queen—wherever and whoever she might be—was indeed their Great Mother who cared for them so overwhelmingly, why did she not visit them? What mother never visited her children, only sent messengers with rigid instructions: this bit can be yours, but the rest is mine forever? She had paid her Hudson's Bay Company "child" money for rights the Company didn't have, but how could she claim the land was hers when his People knew the Creator had given it to them?

Since before the story memory of their oldest Elders, People had lived and hunted on this earth. They belonged here; it was their home, they were this earth's family. It was impossible to give away the Creator's gift by making "treaty," especially with someone whom no one, not even her commissioners, had ever seen. Just because she said it was her land and, if you said it wasn't, she would send thousands of her Young Men with guns and take it? That was no mother. That was a war chief.

McDougall explained none of this. He simply repeated, "You are, like me, children of the Queen. We are all of the same blood; the same God made us and the same Queen rules over us. And these are the presents she sends you. Don't worry, her commissioners will come next summer."

Finally McDougall seemed to be finished. Every eye in Big Bear's council circle met his, and everyone agreed. Elderly and dignified as he was, respected by many Plains Cree and Saulteaux and Assiniboine and Siksika and Blood and Peigan, the Reverend George McDougall could explain nothing because he was simply carrying a message. No one debates with a messenger; you give him a message to carry back. So Big Bear did that:

> "We have heard your words, now here are ours. We want none of the Queen's presents. When we set a fox-trap we scatter pieces of meat all around, but when the fox gets into the trap, we knock him on the head. We want no bait. Let your chiefs come like men and talk to us."

McDougall's expression changed when Big Bear shifted so sharply from *Queen* to *fox-trap*; but what could he do? He reported to Morris that one senior Cree chief, Mista-wasis, had said, "My heart is full of gratitude" for the government message and that Sweetgrass's son had happily accepted all the presents for his father, who was away hunting. But Big Bear was not "reasonable in his demands" and "for years has been regarded as a troublesome fellow." After quoting the chief's exact words in response, he explained that the man was actually a Saulteaux. The Saulteaux were known as "shrewd men" and "mischief makers" and, he added, "the Cree would have driven them out of camp long ago, but were afraid of their medicine, as they are noted conjurors."

If Big Bear had heard this report, he would have pointed out that the Cree wanted to drive him out so badly that he now had the largest Plains Cree following, larger than the senior Sweetgrass. McDougall visited twenty-two bands and estimated their population as 3,976; he did not mention that 600 of them called Big Bear chief.

Vast numbers of buffalo had to give their bodies for such a large band to live, and it was the respectful skill of Big Bear's hunters that provided food from the scattered herds. The police had arrested or chased the whisky traders and wolfers back to Montana, which helped everyone not to waste their hunts on liquor. But the herds were so small now, and skittish, that Big Bear sometimes could only pray for mercy, especially for the little children trusting their parents for the happy life they lived so unawares. And he loved them all, particularly his grandchildren and baby son Horsechild, when they gathered in his lodge and he told them winter stories until they laughed for happiness with him. But it was impossible to listen to a story when hunger tore at them, when their beautiful faces were pulled gaunt like aged spectres. O Great Spirit, pity us. O Buffalo Spirit, be merciful.

That winter (1875–76) they did not take the long trail north to Jackfish Lake, nor even to Fort Pitt. For the first time they wintered in the south among the willows and cottonwoods of The Forks valleys, where they hunted with great care the buffalo, deer, antelope, and other animals sheltering along the two rivers. They traded as little pemmican as possible for ammunition and tea, keeping everything for their own food and clothing, and then, as winter blizzards swept over them, they were safe in their circled lodges with plenty of wood for fires. And they heard again about George McDougall.

He and his son John were building a mission on the Bow River and, needing food, the men rode out along Nose Creek. On a snow-whipped day, they killed six buffalo. The older McDougall rode back alone to their camp, but when John and the others arrived later, his father was not there. Everyone in the area, Blackfoot and Métis and police at Fort Calgary, helped search; first they found his horse and, after thirteen days, his body. As John told the story: "I saw the position in which he had frozen and I thought, Just like him; thoughtful of others even at his last moment. Feeling death was upon him, he had picked a spot as level as he could and laid himself out straight upon it, and crossing his hands, prepared himself to die. His face was perfectly natural." The mourners carried him back to the mission and buried him dressed in his buffalo-hunting clothes above the frozen Bow River.

When he heard, Big Bear remembered why he respected the missionary: he lived what he was, a true, bearded White. Sadly, he had not been born a Person.

About the time McDougall died, Big Bear and a few of his band were at Pitt trading for winter ammunition when they met their first Queen's police. Inspector Paddy Crozier had bristles sticking out wide under his beaked nose. He explained he had been sent to give presents to the Plains Cree and to tell them not to interfere with workers surveying for telegraph and railroad lines, that commissioners were coming this summer (1876) to talk treaty. Big Bear answered, as Crozier reported to Ottawa, that all the Plains People had already heard this, several times, and that "they wished to take nothing from government until the treaty was made."

Crozier peered at him sharply, his whiskers lifting as though he could not quite understand what James Simpson translated. Then he said, The Blackfoot complain to us you Cree are squeezing them off their buffalo lands, back against the mountains and Montana.

Big Bear laughed. We have made peace with the Blackfoot, everyone just wants to live. The Blackfoot should thank you for making their rivers flow faster, dumping all that whisky into the water.

Crozier laughed too. They do thank us, and they're getting fat, eating better.

Big Bear said, But there are still Americans with long Sharps rifles coming north. When they find buffalo, they sit all day on a hill shooting, then they rip off the hides and leave good meat to rot. Why don't police stop them?

There's no law against shooting buffalo and taking hides.

What is "law" for?

To protect everyone.

Then there should be a law stopping sharp-shooters. How many hides went to Montana last season?

Crozier pondered. Maybe two hundred thousand. You Cree sent plenty of them.

Every hide we trade, we eat all the meat.

But soon, Crozier said carefully, there will never be enough buffalo again. Some chiefs are growing food, out of the ground, and maybe more Cree should do that. There is very good food in the ground.

Yes, grass for animals to grow and give their meat to People. If Pakan and Mista-wasis want missionary potatoes and wheat, good, but my People, Little Pine's People, are hunters. We don't sit in one place waiting for food to poke out of the ground.

Crozier nodded as Simpson finished, looking over the log walls of Fort Pitt at the high banks across the North Saskatchewan folded into snow. He said, Sweetgrass, this winter, he's thinking about potatoes too.

When Big Bear did not respond, Crozier continued, My assignment is to tell all Plains People about treaty.

I know … but *we* need to talk with commissioners.

Crozier remained stubborn; he would travel everywhere in such a hard winter. There was in him something beyond McDougall, a rigidity of orders, eyes fixed as if seeing only one spot at a great distance—where he would go.

Crozier is bull-headed Irish, Simpson told Big Bear over a last cup of tea. A trained soldier, he obeys orders even if they are stupid.

They say these are police, not soldiers.

Yes, but about orders they're the same. They do what they're told.

If all police are like Crozier, Big Bear thought, what will happen to them on the blazing winter prairie?

At sunrise the Cree left Pitt for The Forks. The sun burned blue in the sky, light falling like ice in the fierce cold, and they were forced to shield themselves from blindness by cutting slits in buffalo hide for eye patches. Next day the Neutral Hills emerged in the west, with The Nose a hump on the horizon beyond them, sacred places, Ribstone Creek and Battle River and Iron Creek and the high hill where once the Iron Stone had rested—land everywhere as familiar to Big Bear as the palm of the hand nearest his heart. He rode, continuing his prayer for guidance.

They crossed Eye Hill Creek and set their night camp beside the ice of Sounding Lake. When the fire burned in their travelling lodge, Horsechild crawled into his father's lap. The chief folded him in his arms and told him the story of that place, so the little boy would remember it from before he could speak.

"When the Creator made the world, he showed People food for every season. The sweet sap inside poplar bark in spring. Turnip roots to cook in summer. Prairie-rose hips for chewing after their sweet petals fall. And berries, from early summer to late fall, buffalo beans, strawberries, blueberries, saskatoons, choke, and pincherries—that was very good. But the Creator knew winter snow was coming, and People would starve unless they had meat.

"So, hidden deep under water in the ground, the Creator made herds of buffalo. He said to them, 'People living on earth are hungry. If you are kind and give them your meat to eat, I promise that you will always have many strong calves.'

"And the buffalo cried, 'Oh, yes, yes!' and they began to run, charging upward to the light and air. It was here by this lake they came up for us, bursting out of the ground from under the water. And the sound of their coming was like the mighty thunder of Thunderbird, rolling. That is why we call this water Sounding Lake."

And next morning there were tracks in the snow past their lodge. No one had heard a sound, not a dog had barked nor a horse whinnied, but the huge tracks with their five great claws came up from the ice of the lake and went south over the hills in the rising light. Bear had visited them, but had not stopped.

As they travelled south along Sounding Creek, Big Bear sensed he should vow to give a Thirst Dance, asking for guidance. The Queen's commissioners were coming to talk treaty, and he had heard that so far all five treaties said exactly the same things. Was it possible to live with such agreements into a better future than these relentless cycles of disease and hunger and suffering and endless desperation about buffalo? Every spring there were fewer little calves on the prairie bunting their gaunt mothers. The great bulls wandered alone, as if longing to hide in some crevice where there were no bone piles to stumble over, no horned skulls with ridged eye-holes staring at them. Bear, can I dare to make the most difficult prayer for guidance? Will you help my People help me fulfill it?

Once before, after he was asked to become chief, the Cree People had gathered to his vow. But now, after such a hard winter, could he ask Sweetgrass and Little Pine and the other bands to join him for this communal prayer? Would the Creator grant enough buffalo for them to live together and pray and dance and sing and tell stories and give gifts so they could be truly happy? Happy as all People are, at every Thirst Dance, when at last the Thunderbird honours your fasting, thirsting days of prayer with the blessing of rain? And then a magnificent feast, food enough for everyone?

There were great trees along the rivers at The Forks, strong enough for a centre pole for the largest Thirst Dance Lodge, there were more than enough buffalo skulls for ceremony and cloths for offerings … but do I have the strength to be guided. Do I dare? Bear?

On the fourth day they saw Bull's Forehead Hill rising white over The Forks, and they came down into the circle of home to cries of welcome and singing. Several days later a family arrived from the west and told them of McDougall's death. Then a Young Man came from Little Pine's band, wintering in the Hand Hills. He told them Crozier had gone crazy while giving them his message; they had to tie him down or he would walk into the night wearing only under- wear, barefoot in the snow. Police Boss Macleod had ordered eight police to bring him to Fort Macleod.

Messengers. Crozier walking naked into night snow, but not freezing on the prairie like McDougall. Perhaps the Queen's police had more power than a missionary. There were certainly many more of them, in every Company post, and even more in the far south where the Blackfoot had always burned everything White. But Red Cloud, senior chief of the Blood, had given Macleod permission to build his headquarters on an island in the Oldman River, a fort with a hundred police and horses and four huge cannons.

Big Bear had ignored missionaries all his life, but with police that might be impossible. Was that the track message Bear had given him at Sounding Lake after he talked with his first policeman: a warning for the future?

Spring came with a last chinook blowing warm as summer, but there were no herds for a Thirst Dance. That guidance had been given, and so the band moved up the twisting Red Deer River as the frogs—good for eating—sang in marshes and oxbows, and hunted nesting geese and pelicans, the swans and cranes flying north. Scouts searched the horizon from every knob and butte, in every creek bed or coulee. The hunters with Big Bear rode west until they climbed through Old Man's Bed onto the crown of the Wintering Hills, but in half a day they saw nothing, so they continued south around Dead Horse Lake. Soon the ravines of the Bow River cut below them, its water bright as sky flowing from the glacial mountains. Nothing but bleached skeletons in three days' hard riding. They looked at one another, then without a word rode down. They forded the river on a ridge under the water so clear that their horses had no need to swim. The horses grappled up the muddy bank, and they dismounted, deeper in Blackfoot country than any Cree should dare, but if they found buffalo near the river—well—they would then decide if they could risk the women coming across to butcher them.

Big Bear looked down. Beside his moccasin was a small bump in the river mud. He bent, probed with his fingers, and suddenly he knew what he was touching. He washed the stone in a spot of water and its white grain emerged: it bent around to two back legs, curved forward over a white shoulder hump and under a nose to grey front bumps. As wide as his left hand. *Iniskim*, the Blackfoot called this: buffalo stone.

He clenched his fist, and power gathered in him hard and tight as his heart hammering. He could not believe what had been given him, but he had to. He was hiding it in his hand. He glanced at his men; they had all remounted, even Imasees, vigilant and alert to the water—the immense valley and the two river lines of horizon lying empty along the sky. He need explain nothing.

They fanned out on the high prairie, avoiding ridges so as not to appear on the skyline. But while they rode, Big Bear recognized that the highest hill, which in the deceptive level light at first seemed to be a distant butte, was actually a very close, massive rock cairn.

Thousands of stones mounded into a dome, its centre level with a mounted man's waist. Most of the stones were the size of a human head, and lines of them radiated out like the roof rafters of a Blackfoot sundance lodge from its centre pole. The lines ended at his horse's hooves, in a neck-lace of single stones that circled around the central cairn. Sky and land cut deep to the shining river: every offered rock a prayer.

Slowly he rode around the west curve, and his men fol-lowed, riding wide, not a horse stepping inside the stones. There were small cairns in the outer ring, creating lines across the centre that pointed east and west, and then the ring opened south: two lines of large stones widening out over the prairie until they disappeared, as if marking the drive lanes for herding and chasing the stampeding buffalo into a pound or over a cliff. For generations People had acted their prayers here, petitioning the Buffalo Spirit to come, come, pity us, help us live, help us kill your animals.

Imasees was signalling: his son did not want them clus-tered together on the skyline. Big Bear signalled back and his hunters scattered, searching again.

Suddenly Big Bear could not endure the height of his horse; he had to slip off, fold his legs and sit, feel the ground where the driving lane opened the circle. The glacial stones piled together by People for millennia mounded up before him as if resting on the horizon, the prairie dimpled by knobs and hollows, and he felt the weight of the dead in his lifetime, dead by disease and guns and starvation and whisky and raids and attacks and war—the Cree had made war at the Oldman River, and White police had marched in and built their fort within half a day's ride of the battle place— he had helped make war, too often, and left the dead of his People mutilated and rotting in the sun like buffalo slaughtered for nothing but hides. The buffalo stone burned in his hand, all the dead, the dead, and now the Whites an unstoppable flood and he stared at the magnificent cairn floating on the horizon before him while his body simmered with *Buffalo ... trust the buffalo*.

Imasees rode up the driving lane, and Big Bear looked at him. His son said, We found them, on our side of the river. A small herd.

Ahhhhh, Big Bear said and lifted himself to his feet. He walked between the lanes to the cairn and offered up the buffalo stone, *Iniskim*, between rocks level with his eye. Then he and his son together rode down a ravine dusted white as snow by saskatoons blooming and across the river, back to the buffalo.

CHAPTER FIVE

The Rope of Treaty Six

Lieutenant-Governor Alexander Morris required two weeks to haul himself and a large party up the Carlton Trail from Red River to the North Saskatchewan. On Friday, August 18, 1876, the scarlet-coated police band with their tootling trumpets surrounded the royal blue and gold uniforms of the commissioners riding over the river hills above Carlton, where the huge Grandmother flag flipped open in the gentle wind. After half an hour of Cree drumming and dancing and singing, their full-feathered chiefs approached Morris with their pipe presentation. The pipe was, as he later wrote, "… stroked by our hands. After the stroking had been completed, the Indians sat down in front of the council tent, satisfied that in accordance with their custom we had accepted the friendship of the Cree nation." Morris did not comprehend that the pipe had initiated him into a sacred peace ceremony.

The treaty lay ready, English words on parchment, but it had to be spoken into Cree so the People could hear what it said and talk about it. An uneasiness arose about translators—regarding Peter Erasmus, whom the Cree trusted and had themselves hired, and government men Peter Ballendine and John McKay; the complex tongues of Plains Cree, Woods Cree, and Saulteaux needed to be carefully spoken. But finally Morris could repeat what every missionary had already told them: "My Indian brothers … you are, like me, children of the Queen. We are of the same blood, the same God made us, and the same Queen rules over us. I am her Governor of all these territories, and I am here to speak from her to you … face to face."

He then explained, through the translators, that Treaty Six was exactly the same as Treaty Four, which had already been accepted by the southern plains chiefs last year at Qu'Appelle. To summarize:

- Every band could pick the land they wanted, one square mile per family of five.
- They were promised schools, specific farming and carpentry tools, cattle, $1,500 a year for ammunition and twine, liquor prohibition, and uniforms and medals and flags for chiefs.
- Upon signing, a $12 bonus would be paid to every man, woman, and child.
- Payments of $25 per chief, $15 per headman, and $5 to every Person would be made annually, forever.

In four days of discussion with Morris at Carlton, the leading area chiefs followed the Cree tradition of having younger councillors speak for them first, so that the chiefs could speak later without being embarrassed by having their comments rejected. In his report Morris said nothing about young Poundmaker's speech concerning land, but Peter Erasmus recorded Poundmaker's words in his memoirs:

> "'The governor mentions how much land is to be given us. He says one square mile for each family, he will give us.' And in a loud voice [the councillor] shouted, '*All* this is our land! It isn't a piece of pemmican to be cut off and given in little pieces back to us. It is ours and we will take what we want!'"

The Saulteaux leader Badger had come from Treaty Four and again expressed the concerns he had raised the year before about the huge problems of learning to live by farming. Joseph Thoma spoke for Red Pheasant's band: "In the list of articles [needed to farm], there are many things overlooked. I want to ask for as much as will cover the skin of the people … what you have offered is too little. And when you spoke you mentioned ammunition, I did not hear mention of a gun; we will not be able to kill anything simply by setting fire to powder. I want a gun for each chief and headman and I want ten miles all around the reserve where I may be settled."

To which Morris responded with a curt threat: "What I have offered to you has been accepted before by others more in number than you are. I hold out a full hand to you, and it will be a bad day for you and your children if I have to return and say that the Indians threw away my hand."

And then he added a—perhaps ignorant, certainly deceiving—lie: "I want the Indians to understand that all that has been offered is a gift, and they still have the same mode of living as before."

His "same mode of living" comment was not discussed, though every hunter knew the buffalo herds were shrinking south. Threatened, Red Pheasant repudiated the statement of his councillor. He agreed with senior chiefs Mista-wasis and Ahtah-kakoop (Star Blanket), who, having been influenced by Anglican missionaries for a decade now and having long cultivated gardens, had already decided that their future must be with the treaty. Erasmus recorded that Mista-wasis said nothing during Morris's treaty explanations or in the debate the Cree held among themselves—which lasted all of one day. But toward the evening of that day he did at last rise to his feet:

> "I speak directly to Poundmaker and Badger and those others who object to signing the treaty. Have you anything better to offer our people? I for one think that the Great White Queen Mother has offered us a way of life when the buffalo are no more. Gone they will be before many snows have come to cover our heads or graves if such should be. When the Red Coats came, why did the American traders flee in fear, when before they had shot Blackfoot warriors down like dogs and dragged them to the open plains to rot or be eaten by wolves? It was the [Queen's] power that stands behind those few Red Coats ... and I for one look to the Queen's law to protect our people against the evils of firewater and to stop the senseless wars among our people, and against the Blackfoot. We have been in darkness; the Blackfoot and the others are people as we are. They will starve as we will starve when the buffalo are gone. We will be brothers in misery.... We speak of glory, and our memories are all that is left to feed the widows and

orphans of those who died to attain it.... I for one will take the hand that is offered."

Ahtah-kakoop spoke immediately after Mista-wasis:

"Yes, I have carried the dripping scalps of the Blackfoot on my belt.... We killed each other in continuous wars and in horse stealing, all for the glory we all speak of so freely.... But with the buffalo gone, we will have only the vacant prairie which none of us have learned to use.... Let us show our wisdom by choosing the right path now while we yet have a choice. For my part, I think the Queen Mother has offered us a new way. I will accept her hand for my people."

And next day they both signed, the first Cree chiefs to make their X marks on an English Treaty Six they could not read; they trusted what the translators told them Morris had said was in it. In this way, at Carlton on August 23, 1876, Mista-wasis, Ahtah-kakoop, and seven other chiefs and thirty-six councillors did, in the name of their 1,787 band members then present and the hundreds more hunting on the plains, "cede, release, surrender and yield up to the Government of the Dominion of Canada for Her Majesty the Queen and her successors forever, all their rights, titles and privileges to the lands ... embracing an area of one hundred and twenty-one thousand square miles [312,000 sq. km], be the same more or less...."

Land two and a half times larger than England.

Then, "deeply satisfied," Morris and his party made the money payments and trekked on to present Treaty Six to the second group of Cree bands at Fort Pitt.

Big Bear's band had lived in the Great Sand Hills all summer, hunting as near the American border as Old Man On His Back; despite all the messages they had previously received, in 1876 they heard not a word from Morris. When they did hear, via a message from James Simpson, that the governor was at Pitt with the treaty, Big Bear and several councillors galloped north on their fastest horses with alternates running beside them. They arrived opposite Fort Pitt at dusk on September 12, the day after Indian Commissioner William Christie of Edmonton had finished making treaty payments to all the People assembled there. Sweetgrass, Pakan, and seven other chiefs, with their twenty councillors, had already added their X marks to Treaty Six on September 9, the day before Simpson's frantic messenger had finally found Big Bear's camp and gave him the message: Where are you? Sweetgrass is at Fort Pitt talking treaty!

How could it happen so fast? Big Bear asked Simpson, who was sitting beside him at his night fire. They were under poplars in an east coulee; Big Bear could not yet face crossing the river and meeting those new "treaty-promise chiefs" camped beside Pitt. Sweetgrass was out on the prairie near us just eight days ago.

Simpson said, Morris himself sent for Sweetgrass. And the chief met Morris in his ceremonial suit, took him in his arms, and kissed him on both cheeks.

What!

The other chiefs did that too, and the councillors.

Kiss the governor?

Like Christians after their feast ceremony.... Priests call it drinking the blood and eating the flesh of Jesus, but Methodists say it's just wine and bread—they always kiss afterward.

Ahhhhh.

Simpson said, The governor talked all next day, explaining payment and general starvation rations and such things. Then the Cree held council for one day, and the day after that they made short speeches and signed. On Sunday they had church, and on Monday Christie finished paying the treaty money—everybody, even babies, got twelve dollars for signing—and today Morris packed up; he's leaving.

Lone Man sat studying the fire, but Twin Wolverine glanced at his father for an instant and Big Bear had to look away, through the golden aspen to the bright stars.

Simpson added, The Cree are giving their paper money to the traders. Lots of traders, there's lots of stuff to buy.

Lone Man said, not quite able to believe it, After one day of council ... every chief agreed, about everything?

Yes. Because of Chief Little Hunter and Erasmus, Simpson explained. They reported about Carlton, how Poundmaker and Badger objected to the treaty, and then what Mista-wasis and Ahtah-kakoop advised, why they would sign. And then Sweetgrass said to this council, "I consider those chiefs far wiser than I am. If they have accepted this treaty for their people, after many days of talk and careful thought, then I am ready to accept it for my people."

Big Bear murmured, Many days of talk. The good Sweetgrass, he's almost all Abraham now.

Simpson nodded, Pakan too. He praised Little Hunter and Erasmus by saying, "They would never tell us something that was not for our good. So, if those other chiefs who are greater in number than we are have found this treaty good, I and my headmen will sign."

He's no longer a hard Cree pakan (nut), he's a soft Christian Seenum.

That's how he signed the treaty, James Seenum.

Ahhhhh, said Big Bear. And Sweetgrass?

Weekas-kookee-pay-yin.

Yes, he would give his Cree name away.

So … English, Cree … which name should they use?

No name! Big Bear growled. Not to give away the land!

They were all so silent then that they heard the aspen shiver, the river gurgle beyond the willows. And then the splash of paddles, the rasp of a canoe over sand. In a moment Imasees stepped into the firelight with another Young Man, who nodded to the circle.

Chief Sweetgrass sends you greetings, he said. He says the governor will not travel before he talks to you in the morning.

Thank your chief, Big Bear said. We will come over to meet him at sunrise.

Next morning the treaty chiefs, in their red jackets with silver medals hanging from their necks, walked with Big Bear in his black buffalo robe into the square at Fort Pitt, where, throughout his life, his band had come for ceremonial welcomes and trade. But this ceremony went far beyond any regular summer barter with the Company; Simpson watched from aside, and a small man in a dark blue uniform and the much larger Chief Factor William Christie sat in chairs surrounded by the Queen's scarlet police snorting air out of their curled instruments. The log buildings rattled echoes.

When they were finished, everyone except Sweetgrass seated themselves on the ground facing the governor, and, as Commission Secretary A.G. Jackes recorded: "Sweet Grass [to Lieutenant-Governor Morris]: 'We are all glad to see you here, and we have come to say good-bye….'"

Morris replied with a similar greeting to the treaty chiefs and "The Bear." The other two translators had already left and so John McKay—whose Plains Cree words often got tangled with Woods Cree—was left to fumble through Morris's reply. Then Sweetgrass nodded to Big Bear and sat down.

Silence lengthened, and the governor stirred impatiently. Big Bear looked at him. His face was grey; he seemed ill, and very tired, as if the softest Company bed had not helped him sleep. Morris's blue eyes stared at him unblinkingly, and Big Bear slid his glance aside, beyond the wooden roofs to the unchanging river hills. Jackes continues:

> "Big Bear: 'I find it difficult to speak, because some of the bands are not represented. I have come off to speak for the different bands [Plains Cree and Assiniboine] that are out on the plains.

It is no small matter we were to consult about. I expected the chiefs here would have waited until I arrived.... The people who have not come stand as a barrier before what I would have had to say; my mode of living is hard.'

"Sweet Grass: 'My friend ... I feel as if I saw life when I see the representative of the Queen; let nothing be a barrier between you and him.... Think of our children and those who come after, there is life and succor for them; say yes, and take his hand.'

"[Pakan]: 'We have all taken it, and we think it is for our good.'

"Big Bear: 'Stop, stop, my friends. I have never seen the Governor before; I have seen Mr. Christie many times.... I said ... when I see [the governor] I will make a request that he save me from what I most dread, that is: the rope to be about my neck—hanging, it is not given us by the Great Spirit that the red man or white man should shed each other's blood.'"

No doubt the words Jackes recorded (and Morris also) were what McKay translated; the question is, are they exactly what Big Bear said? For more than a century the Cree oral tradition has cast doubt on their accuracy, and since 1966, historians have questioned their meaning as well. As Dorothy Thunder, sessional lecturer in Cree at the University of Alberta, corroborated in 2008: "Translations into English have always been very complicated as one loses the in-depth/deeper meaning while translating." She then explained that the Cree expression *esakâpekinit* means "I am being led by him/her using a string/rope," but the somewhat similarly pronounced *ehakotiht* means "s/he is being hung by the neck." Did McKay mistake this crucial sound difference or simply not know the expression and added the word "hanging" as an explanation? It would seem that Big Bear's powerful image—after all, he was an orator and a horse-man—of fearing that the treaty would control his life, make him lose his freedom just like a horse can be forcibly led about by a rope around its neck, was mistranslated into an elaboration on the White practice of hanging criminals. Beyond that, since the Cree considered the soul of a person to reside in the nape of the neck, the metaphor of a rope around the neck was even more meaningful to them: it implied destruction of the soul.

While Big Bear spoke to his fellow chiefs, McKay had been translating for Morris. But now, before any other chief could respond, the governor began a harangue. To quote Jackes:

> "Governor: 'It is given us by the Great Spirit, man should not shed his brother's blood, and it was also spoken to us that he who shed his brother's blood, should have his own spilt. No good Indian has the rope about his neck. If a white man killed an Indian, not in self defense, the rope would be put around his neck.... The good Indian need never be afraid; their lives will be safer ... the redcoats, they were here to protect....'"

Big Bear listened to McKay's translation, but could not comprehend why Morris was responding so strangely. He had created a picture for the chiefs of his dread of the treaty controlling him like a roped horse, of it killing him by choking his very soul—but Morris interrupted to lecture them on the White punishment for murder!

So Big Bear tried to explain himself again, to the governor as well as the chiefs:

> "Big Bear: 'What we want is that we should hear what will make our hearts glad, and all good peoples' hearts glad. There were plenty things

left undone, and it does not look well to leave them so.'

"Governor: 'I do not know what has been left undone!'

"Big Bear said he would like to see his people before he acted: 'I have told you what I wish, that there be no [rope around my neck].'

"Governor: 'Why are you so anxious about bad men? The Queen's law punishes murder with death, and your request cannot be granted.'"

And Big Bear realized that, somehow, between what he had said and what the governor understood, something profound had shifted. Perhaps it was McKay struggling with the endless cycle of translation, a struggle Big Bear understood very well from circling among Cree and Saulteaux or Assiniboine or Blackfoot. Once you translated a deep word aloud, it could not be taken back. That word fixed itself in memory, even after you spoke a hundred more to try to explain it. He glanced at Simpson leaning against a house wall. His friend shook his head sadly: nothing to be done about the governor's stubborn thinking.

Neither of them could know that Big Bear's expressions would be unambiguously recorded as "hanged" in Morris's reports and thereby in the government's eyes brand Big Bear as a cowardly man who was fearful that Indians—including himself—would probably commit murders and consequently be condemned to execution under the Queen's law. Clearly a "troublesome, very bad" Indian.

So Big Bear abruptly stopped speaking about treaty control and loss of freedom by turning to another problem.

> "Big Bear: 'Then these chiefs will help us protect the buffalo, that there may be enough for us all. I have heard what has been said, and I am glad we are to be helped. Why do these men not speak?'

> "[Cut Arm]: 'We do not speak, because Sweet Grass has spoken for us all. What he says, we all say.'"

The governor rose, and the chiefs on the ground before him knew the meeting was over. Stumbling, McKay gave them Morris's last, immovable, words.

> "Governor: 'I want The Bear to tell ... the other chiefs [on the plains] what has been done, and that it is for them, as if they were here. Next year they and their people can join the treaty and they will lose

nothing.... The North-West Council is considering
the framing of a law to protect the buffaloes, and,
when they make it, they will expect the Indians to
obey it. The Government will not interfere with the
Indian's daily life, they will not bind him...."'

(Ahhhhh, Big Bear thought, he did understand one thing
about rope ... but how do prairie hunters have a daily life
without buffalo?)

"'They will help him to make a living on reserves
by giving him the means of growing from the soil,
his food. The only occasion when help would be
given, would be if Providence should send a great
famine or pestilence upon the whole Indian
people included in the treaty. We only looked at
something unforeseen and not at hard winters or
the hardship of single bands....

"'And now, I am going away. The country is large,
another governor will be sent in my place. He will
live among you. I trust you will receive him as you
have done me, and give him your confidence....
Indians of the plains ... I never expect to see you
again, face to face.... When I go back to my home

beyond the great lakes, I will often think of you and rejoice to hear of your prosperity. I ask God to bless you, and your children. Farewell.'

"The Indians responded with loud ejaculations of satisfaction … each shook hands with the Governor … elevating his hand as they grasped it, to heaven, and invoking the blessings of the Great Spirit.

"The Bear remained sitting until all had said goodbye to the Governor, and then he rose and taking his hand, said, 'I am glad to meet you. I am alone; but if I had known the time, I would have been here with all my People. I am not an undutiful child, I do not throw back your hand, but as my People are not here, I do not sign. I will tell them what I have heard, and next year I will come.'"

Morris said, tightening his hand, "Yes, come next year with all your people and accept it."

That is not what I said, Big Bear thought. But he knew that for this year words were finished; staring Morris was already in the canoe crossing the river to his carts, already enduring eight hundred miles of prairie horizon that would finally lead him, exhausted, to Red River. Carrying the English Treaty Six with all its X marks to Government. Would the Cree ever see, in their language, everything that had been said here?

He greeted Simpson but could not pause for talk: Sweetgrass and Pakan were waiting with Lone Man, the many Cree lodges set against the valley hills and Young Men riding the skyline. Momentarily he felt that all could still be right in the Creator's world.

Then Sweetgrass spoke beside him, walking, his deep and gentle voice, You remember the letter Christie wrote for us, in Edmonton—now at last they came. I see nothing to fear. Some of us will clear land and learn how to grow food, and we can all, hand in hand, protect the buffalo.

The must of red cloth coats drifted in the autumn air, but Big Bear was thinking land. He asked, How will we keep the land?

Sweetgrass avoided answering directly; he said, Mista-wasis and Ahtah-kakoop already chose theirs, north of the river at Carlton, and One Arrow at Duck Lake.

Pakan added, Red Pheasant wants his place in the Eagle Hills.

All of them far apart, little pieces?

Wherever we want it. You could go to Jackfish Lake, one square mile for every five People.

How much is that, "one square mile"?

Simpson will know.

He would. But it sounded very small. How would you feed hundreds of People on land you could probably walk around in three days? Maybe enough territory for two cow moose and four yearlings, maybe a bull now and then, and once they were killed ... to live year after year, you could not choose one bit of hunting land, and gardens only grew well on certain soil. Abruptly he realized how White he was thinking, and his council voice burst out deep and angry:

One square mile! We belong everywhere here! Big Bear's arms waved to the hills, river, sky. Wherever we lean our lodge-poles together and build a fire, there is our home!

No one said a word; they walked as if their feet together in the grass felt the same Earth memory.

Big Bear said quietly, Three years ago the Americans set aside, for the Blackfoot, the Judith River basin and all land north of the Missouri to the border, from the mountains to east of Poplar River, more than fifteen riding days long. And it's full of buffalo, huge herds.

Sweetgrass nodded. But I also heard White soldiers won't let the Sioux hunt there; they chase and kill them.

If they can find them.

Pakan said, Those Long Knives will never leave the Sioux alone, now that they killed Yellowhair Custer.

Fighting Whites with guns is stupid, Sweetgrass said. Whites have endless soldiers, they never stop shooting, and there are only a limited number of People. That's why we had to make treaty.

Pakan spoke, in his careful way: I told the governor I wanted a big reserve, big enough for all the Plains Cree, from Whitemud River to Dog Rump Creek along the North Saskatchewan River, everything north to the Beaver River.

That might almost be enough land, Big Bear said. But the buffalo are all south of the South Saskatchewan.

Pakan asked, How can Cree live with buffalo when they're all in Blackfoot country?

The Crow hunt mostly at peace in that Blackfoot Missouri country. Maybe we have to decide, do we live with Blackfoot, or do we try to live like Whites.

Maybe, Lone Man offered, all the Plains Cree should take land together, in the south there with the buffalo.

The Cypress Hills? Pakan asked. I've never hunted that far south.

They were near the Sweetgrass lodges; children ran to greet them, and the venerable old chief looked up from his hands and laughed to see them come. While they walked, talking, he had been turning the beautiful rifle Morris had given him for signing the treaty over and over in his hands.

Sweetgrass said, You heard them say it, the Grandmother has big breasts. She'll feed us if starvation comes.

To this day the Cree oral tradition repeats that Fort Pitt breast story. Historian Neal McLeod quotes five different informants who elaborate on this metaphor concerning the iconic mother "who would provide for the Indians as the earth once had." Isabel Smallboy was alive when the treaty was signed and said it most directly: "The Queen's tits are very big and you will never eat them all, that's how rich they are."

Whether or not Queen Victoria ever heard the story is not known.

CHAPTER SIX

Last Chief of the Free Plains Cree

That winter, Big Bear's camp below Bull's Forehead Hill at The Forks grew to a hundred lodges—eight hundred People. And in January 1877, a message arrived to tell them Chief Sweetgrass was dead. Killed by his Morris rifle—accidentally perhaps, because it was in the hands of his brother-in-law when it fired. A beautiful rifle that weighed almost nothing and needed only a copper cartridge; you simply slipped it into the breech and touched the trigger.

The messenger travelled through the hard drifts with his own and three other families. They told Big Bear, Sweetgrass is gone. You are our chief now.

By summer, when it was time to ride to talk treaty again, there were more than a thousand People in his band. But so many could not travel over land covered with nothing but bones, and neither Little Pine nor Bobtail nor Piapot, all hunting in the south, wanted to talk to a governor. They asked Big Bear to ride to Pitt with as many councillors as wanted to go.

The gathered council advised him: Chief Sweetgrass followed the advice of White priests and gave away our greatest gift, the land, and so quickly his soul walks with the dead. You have given away nothing. Speak for our Plains People, to keep us free on the land and protect the buffalo, especially from the Sioux.

Big Bear had eight days of prairie riding to pray for the wisdom he would need to lighten the Grandmother's heavy hand. The land must remain, and also the buffalo: if they were hunted respectfully, People could live. But Piapot had reported that the two thousand Sioux under Four Horns and Sitting Bull, who had fled American soldiers by crossing the border, were now killing every buffalo near Wood Mountain. No animals would escape them to go north in their usual summer migration—how could buffalo survive, hunted like that? Or the northern Cree? O Great Spirit, pity us, O Only One, hear us.

But there was nothing to discuss at Fort Pitt anyway. The new governor, David Laird, was far away talking treaty at Blackfoot Crossing, and he simply sent an assistant to make payments to the fifteen hundred hungry Cree waiting for him. If you were on the treaty list, M.G. Dickieson gave you five dollars. If you signed for the first time, he gave you twelve dollars, but he could not change one word of the treaty, nor talk about it. Also, a Buffalo Ordinance had been passed: no hunting of cows from November to August, no hunting of calves all year.

How, Big Bear asked, could the People on the prairie stay alive with such a law? Buffalo must be hunted only by Plains People, not by Sioux or Whites. But no, the ordinance applied to everyone, no exceptions.

Simpson said in disgust, I'm leaving this miserable place. There's nothing to trade, a clerk just hands out money, and I.G. Baker drags big carts from Benton and sells crap nobody needs. I'm going east to breed horses.

So Big Bear could ask him: Why did you sign Treaty Six?

Simpson exclaimed, You heard that? I signed as a witness, I saw your chiefs make their X marks.

But the Great Spirit gave you the land too, through your grandmother.

Simpson laughed. You sound like Louis Riel! Too bad he had to run to the States to stay alive.

Strangely, via messenger David Laird readily accepted Big Bear's request that the 1878 treaty payments, and discussion, should take place at Sounding Lake, nearer the non-treaty

People hunting on the southern prairie. It came to Big Bear that perhaps the government was no longer concerned about Plains Cree refusals; after all, on September 22, 1877, Laird had talked the entire Blackfoot Confederacy into signing Treaty Seven, surrendering forever the remainder of the prairies not already yielded up in Treaties One, Two, Four, and Six. Crowfoot's X led the long list of Blood, Peigan, Stoney, and Sarcee leaders.

Big Bear knew every prairie treaty was essentially the same. With this final treaty signed, changing a White word in any one of them would be harder than ever.

That winter was mild, but by spring 1878, those Cree living on small, measured treaty lands faced starvation. What little garden food they had grown with few tools and no experience didn't last half the winter; they had no mills to grind their sparse grain and there were almost no animals to hunt. Nevertheless, Laird declared there was no "general famine throughout the land" and that therefore he need do nothing. What could they do?

When the leaves came out, People trekked south from Carlton, from Jackfish and Saddle and Frog lakes, from Edmonton and the Peace Hills until more than three thousand People crowded into The Forks valleys with Big Bear's band. There were festivals of dancing and food, Elders told

Wîsahkêcâhk stories that Horsechild had never heard, and children's laughter spread under the cottonwoods to the sandbanks of the ice-running river. But to feed themselves they had to move to the buffalo, south, so deep into Blackfoot territory that the great cones of the Sweetgrass Hills floated grey as dreams on the horizon.

They look like animals, Imasees said, waiting for us. Why don't we go live there? Just follow the Milk River.

It's Long Knives country, said Twin Wolverine.

If the Sioux come to this side of the Line and kill our buffalo, we can go there and kill theirs.

The Long Knives would shoot us.

Sayos and her daughter Nowakich were roasting buffalo haunch over the lodge fire. Nowakich's husband, Lone Man, chewed meat, saying nothing, and suddenly she spoke: Maskepetoon had a big silver medal from their Great Father, like Sweetgrass got from the Grandmother. Does that mean Maskepetoon made treaty with the Whites over there?

Yes, he had a medal, Big Bear said. That "Father's" face was on it too.

Who cares, a dead silver face. Imasees rose, belching comfortably. You can't even see their stupid Line, it's wherever Whites say it is. I say, if we're strong enough to ride on the prairie, it's our land.

Once that had certainly been true, but no longer. Big Bear contemplated that as he cantered north with several councillors while their Young Men searched the prairie ahead. They had only two hundred miles of steady riding to Sounding Lake, but most of the treaty People remained hunting with his. They knew that five dollars gave you one thin blanket or half a bag of mouldy flour; one buffalo, with liver and brain and heart and tongue and nose and intestines and hooves and horns and bones and mounds of meat and a huge hide, made mockery of a little pile of paper.

Nevertheless, two thousand Cree now living on reserves of "land set aside" waited for the governor on the flats where Sounding Creek entered the lake. Stone-faced David Laird arrived on August 13 with his troop of police surrounding the money-chest wagons. As Laird reported it, Big Bear immediately stated his most direct demand:

> "'The Great Spirit has supplied us with plenty of buffalo for food until the white man came. Now as that means of support is about to fail us, the Government ought to take the place of the Great Spirit, and provide us with the means of living in some other way.'"

In three days of talk, Laird conceded nothing. He described Big Bear as an "old [he was fifty-three] and weazened" man whom he disliked intensely because "he was an untrustworthy and bad Indian." In any case, the Canadian prairie had been signed away by most of the plains chiefs: what did a few hard-line Cree matter, even if their bands numbered some thousands? Let them eat buffalo, wait them out.

The White wife of a trader certainly did not consider Big Bear "weazened." She wrote:

> "He was to be seen every day riding round the camp on an Indian pony, haughty and defiant, his face and body adorned with war paint and his long black hair decorated with eagle feathers.... He was the typical red Indian in all his savage glory and was a striking figure, with his brown body well tanned by the sun exposed to view...."

Together with the treaty chiefs, who delayed accepting their annual payments because living on reserves was proving so disastrous, Big Bear argued that the government had added crucial living clauses of extra food to Treaties One and Two, and therefore Treaty Six must be augmented as well to deal with the deadly sudden loss of the buffalo.

Laird remained adamant: he could add nothing. When Cree Young Men galloped around his circled wagons in protest, firing shots into the air, he threatened them with arrest.

On Monday, August 25, 1878, the first issue of the *Saskatchewan Herald*, handset and printed by P.G. Laurie at Battleford, now the capital of the North-West Territories, reported that Big Bear spoke "not only for himself and his band, but for those who had already signed" and that "he would come again next year to receive the answer."

The first newspaper west of Red River had half its information wrong. Big Bear did not mention coming again next year, and part of the reason was Sounding Lake. The shallow water so beautiful in its surround of shaggy Neutral Hills, which the Cree and Blackfoot had once dedicated as a peace boundary between them, the lake where, their stories told them, the buffalo had burst up from the hand of the Creator—this doubly sacred place. The wind shifting in the wolf willow whispered his prayer back to him: *Trust the buffalo*. To face Whites he needed the resolute courage of that faith, and the wisdom of time to understand what The Only One wanted People to do. Out of three annual attempts to talk treaty and now three days of deadlock with Laird at Sounding Lake grew a conviction, and a vow.

He told Laird he would watch for four Cree years to see how Government kept faith with those Cree who had signed Treaty Six. For four years his band, and every Person who wanted to join them, would watch and live the independence and freedom they had always had: with buffalo, without treaty.

Four years. Had Big Bear's band been Blood or Siksika, an Elder would have focused his memory of those years in the cryptic oral code of the Blackfoot Winter Count. The Cree, however, had highly respected Old Men who were "professional rememberers" for their communities; they could recount, with practised accuracy, key tribal events of the near and distant past. The band's Old Men might have remembered those four years with these happenings:

Year One: August (Buffalo Breeding Moon) 1878 to August 1879

When Little Pine and Lucky Man Signed

- *Saskatchewan Herald*, November 16: Government surveyors staking land near the Bow and Oldman rivers are confronted by Assiniboine, who tell them they "know of no one in Canada who has a right to take away their land." Big Bear is sent for, and a parley results in dead-lock. When Police Commissioner Irvine arrives from Fort Walsh with twenty-six police, he finds three hun-dred Assiniboine, Blackfoot, Cree, and Sioux warriors waiting. Big Bear and Irvine agree that the surveyors will stop their work and the Indians and police will "leave the dispute to be settled between the Governor and Big Bear when the leaves come out." There is no mention of Big Bear wearing his war Bear paw.

- Few fall buffalo and early snow with weakened horses make hunting barely possible. The Eagle Hills People are so near starvation that they petition officials to give them next summer's treaty payments in January. They receive nothing.

- Father Lestanc with the Métis at The Forks writes to the *Herald* on March 24: "Very severe winter. All the tribes— the Sioux, Blackfoot, Bloods, Sarcees, Assiniboines, Stoneys, Cree and Saulteaux—now form but one party, having the same mind. Big Bear up to this time cannot be accused of uttering a single objectionable word, but the fact of his being the head and soul of all our Canadian plain Indians leaves room for conjecture. They also seem desirous of securing Sitting Bull's assistance to obtain another, and better, treaty." But on May 5, the *Herald* reports: "The great confederacy of which Big Bear was to be the chief has come to nothing. The Blackfoot declined to give him their allegiance, actuated perhaps by a lingering remembrance of past enmity. The large party that wintered at The Forks has now dispersed."

- Prime Minister Macdonald appoints his friend Edgar Dewdney as the new Indian Commissioner. Arriving at Fort Walsh via Montana, Dewdney notes:

  "July 2: Had an interview with some non-Treaty Cree Indians. They are said to have cut themselves off from Big Bear, although they deny it.

  "July 3: Had interview with Big Bear and other Indians that promised to take the Treaty. Little Pine [270 persons] and Lucky Man [200 persons] did so, leaving Big Bear almost alone.

  "July 4: Had long interview with Big Bear but no results. The same—talk but would not take the Treaty. Parted good friends."

Dewdney writes to Macdonald confidentially: "I have not formed such a poor opinion of Big Bear as some appear to have done. He is a very independent character, self-reliant, and appears to know how to make his own living without begging from the government."

Year Two: August 1879 to August 1880

When the Buffalo Disappeared across the Line

- At Sounding Lake, Dewdney pays Little Pine's band and those who signed with Big Bear's councillor Lucky Man—Imasees's father-in-law—the twelve-dollar signing bonus plus another fifteen dollars for three years' back pay. Little Pine trades and leaves immediately to hunt buffalo.

- A number of Big Bear's band—which still numbered more than two thousand People—make the long trek with him to Fort Pitt carrying their few hides. It will be their last free trade on the North Saskatchewan; bleached bones cover the prairie, and they realize that whatever living animals remain have disappeared into Montana. Police Commissioner James Macleod writes Ottawa that increased American military manoeuvres along the border, including deliberate grass fires, are preventing the usual buffalo migration into Canada.

- Big Bear's band lives that winter in Montana, hunting along the Milk River and into the Bears Paw Mountains. Louis Riel is trying to organize a Métis-Indian coalition to possibly invade Canada and invites Big Bear to visit the Big Bend Métis settlement. The chief stays one day and, as his grandson Four Souls remembered it in 1975, tells Riel: "Let's fight the Queen with her law, not with guns. This way we might have a chance." Riel notes in his papers: "The Cree have a very good chief. He is Big Bear. He is a man of good sense."

- Fort Benton *Record*, March 12: Five thousand starving Indians from Canada's northern reserves are camped around Fort Walsh and existing on sparse rations distributed by police. "There is nothing whatever to keep them from starvation north of the line."

During treaty payments at Battleford in July, Poundmaker speaks for all the emaciated People just returned from Fort Walsh. He tells Dewdney the Cree are weak, without provisions, and that they need more resources to farm their reserves. "I am not asking for more money. We need ten cows and ten yokes of cattle on each reserve because now, when one family works with one yoke, lots of others must remain idle and we cannot put in much crop. If we get what we ask, I think we can make our living out of the ground. The Cree that are not settled are watching us."

Dewdney responds: "Poundmaker is very sensible; when Indians talk that way, the government is much more likely to assist them than when they use threats." Within weeks Dewdney officially names Poundmaker a chief, and he and 182 followers take a reserve along Cutknife Hill on the Battle River. But more cows and oxen never appear.

- *Saskatchewan Herald,* August 2: It seems Wandering Spirit has ridden from Montana to observe the new commissioner in Battleford. Big Bear's war chief declares: "I am very happy at what Poundmaker has said. I intend to abide by it." Not long after, he is again hunting buffalo with Big Bear across the Line.

Year Three: August 1880 to August 1881

When Cree and Blackfoot Lived Together

- Crowfoot's starving treaty Siksika settle near Carrol, Montana, and pledge peace with Big Bear's twenty-four hundred Plains Cree. They live side by side that winter and hunt the buffalo still plentiful in the Judith basin. Good meat and hides are available, but also endless whisky, and that creates havoc. As trader James Schultz later wrote:

  "There were nights when a thousand Indians would be drunk together, dancing and singing around little fires built down in the timber, some crying foolishly, some making love, others going through all kinds of strange and uncouth antics. But there was very little quarrelling among Big Bear's people, not half a dozen being killed in the whole winter. More than that number froze to death, falling on their way home in the night."

- A band member has a sexual affair with Big Bear's youngest wife and, in a drunken rage, clubs the chief to death. But, as his grandson Four Souls told it later, "Big Bear's oldest wife, Sayos, had been instructed what to do in case he got killed. So she called a medicine man who followed the instructions and Big Bear was brought back to life. He didn't take revenge on this man right away, but later he got the medicine man to use bad medicine on him and killed him." And Big Bear forgives his young wife because of the alcohol.

- In mid-February, the bands from Mosquito, Moosomin, and Poundmaker—now "the most influential chief on the Saskatchewan"—come to Battleford to declare they must hold a Grand Council with the Indian Commissioner. The treaty understandings must be changed, Poundmaker states; if extra rations are not given, he will kill government oxen for food, and there are not police enough to arrest him. But there is no commissioner in winter Battleford, nor even an agent, to answer them, and they return to their bits of "land set aside" all the hungrier.

- In May, Poundmaker and three thousand treaty Cree, unable to plant crops because they have no seed or draft

animals or food, leave their reserves again to look for
buffalo in the Cypress Hills. But no herds will ever again
roam free in prairie Canada. To prevent violence, the
Fort Walsh police dole out starvation rations of flour and
rancid bacon hauled from Fort Benton, before they force
the People north for treaty payments. Meanwhile,
Montana ranchers petition the U.S. Army to chase
Canadian Indians back over the border because, though
they are "ostensibly here for the purpose of hunting buffalo, they have killed and eaten many of our cattle."

Year Four: August 1881 to August 1882

When Big Bear Ran His Last Buffalo

• The Marquis of Lorne, Governor General of Canada,
tours the North-West Territories. Poundmaker guides his
huge party from Battleford across the bone-haunted
prairie to Crowfoot on the Bow River. During the journey Poundmaker is astounded to discover that the
haughty, aloof Imperial Head of Canada, whose one wife
is the daughter of the Great Grandmother venerated in
every treaty, can actually explain nothing about government actions. The man Macdonald, who will never visit
the Territories and whom no more than a dozen Plains

People will ever see, makes all decisions as Head of Indian Affairs through an Indian Act no Person has ever heard a word about.

- Another hard winter. There are still large herds along the Missouri, but rotgut whisky is more destructive than ever, and cycles of horse stealing by Young Men ruin the peace. Big Bear and his People, camped on the Musselshell River, recognize that despite adequate hunting, their life and community are being destroyed.

- Major John Young, in charge of the immense Indian lands along the Missouri, offers Big Bear a reservation if he signs a treaty with Washington. Twin Wolverine, Imasees, and Wandering Spirit are strongly in favour, and a deep rift develops in the band when Big Bear will not agree.

- In March, the U.S. Army launches "The Milk River Sweep." Soldiers attack Little Pine's band and harry them back across the border, but a messenger warns Big Bear in the Little Rocky Mountains, and war chief Wandering Spirit takes command. He sends scouts to watch for patrols while camp is struck and, covering their trail of travois and hoof prints, twelve hundred People disappear into the Missouri Breaks. The Benton *Record* is disgusted: the army should present Big Bear the "Freedom of Milk River" on a silver platter—if they can find him.

But the Plains Cree cannot live a life in hiding. After one more good hunt, and some warrior adventures for the Young Men stealing back horses stolen from them in past years, as the leaves open on the Missouri cottonwoods, Big Bear's band trails slowly north. Past the valley where Chief Joseph and his Nez Percé made their last stand in the Bears Paw Mountains, north along Battle Creek, across the Medicine Line and past Old Man On His Back to the Cypress Hills. They circle their lodges at Cypress Lake; a day's ride away, near Fort Walsh among the green-grass hills are the destitute camps of five thousand treaty Indians. After four years of difficult independence, of watching and waiting, Big Bear and his People have returned to ignored promises, impossible farming conditions, and starvation. From the northern reserves around the Peace Hills, named to honour Chief Maskepetoon, Chiefs Bobtail, Ermineskin, and Samson have sent a bitter letter to Macdonald:

"The conditions of the treaty were mutually agreed to. We understood them to be inviolable and in the presence of the Great Spirit reciprocally binding. But alas! how simple we were.… We are now reduced to the lowest stage of poverty. We were once a proud and independent people, and now we are mendicants at the door of every white man in the country, and if it were not for the charity of white settlers, we should all die on government fare.... Our young women are reduced by starvation to become prostitutes to the white man for a living, a thing unheard of before amongst ourselves. What shall we then do?.... Shall we still be refused [assistance] and be compelled to adhere to the conclusion that the treaty is a farce enacted to kill us quietly, and if so, let us die at once?"

At Fort Walsh in July, Police Commissioner Irvine forces the People to go north for their treaty payments by withholding all rations. As Indian Farm Instructor Robert Jefferson later commented: "The Indians were more law-abiding than white men under the same circumstances would ever have been; had it been otherwise, ten times the number of police would not have kept them in order."

THE RUNNING HOOVES DRUMMED Big Bear into another country, calling and calling, as the buffalo effortlessly fanned out before him. The gashed wounds left in the animals' flanks by hunters they had once and then again outrun dripped brilliant red in the rhythmic bunch and release of their muscles, and then there was only one great cow running, floating strong, growing large until beside him streamed the tufted stick of her tail, the rolling leap of muscle in her hindquarters, and he felt life surge within her, her heart in that violent, happy thunder as she ran true the great curve of Earth, as he drifted along her flank, and for an instant his arrow pointed her, one instant and its feathers burst in the coarse hair behind her shoulder. And her rhythm rippled momentarily, her heart staggered as his arrow feathers flamed into double blossom. Then his horse had to swing sharply aside or he would have pitched over her, falling.

He stood where her magnificent head furrowed the ground and he prayed, asking forgiveness of the Buffalo Spirit for this death, giving thanks for the life that had thereby been granted. And saw a coyote standing on a rise beyond her, mouth open, laughing. And he also saw what Coyote was laughing at: a fountain of blood growing out of the ground like a hideous prairie lily opening upward, and he stretched out his hands to stop that. But it burst between his fingers, higher, he would never be able to squash it back into the earth, while Coyote on another rise now stood laughing, mouth open. As his whole world changed to blood.

CHAPTER SEVEN

Signing the Treaty

It was all very well for Indian Commissioner Dewdney to write his friend the prime minister in 1879 that "Big Bear is a very independent character, self-reliant …," but there was no independence, no self-reliance for prairie People without buffalo. By 1876, everyone knew the buffalo were in drastic decline. But no one anticipated that the animals would disappear from Canada within three years, nor that the U.S. Army would build two more military posts, increase border patrols, and deliberately stop the annual buffalo migration north to save the last animals for their own Native Peoples. And the Ottawa government's blithe assumption that, within two years, Aboriginal hunters could transform themselves into self-sufficient farmers on northern prairies where well-equipped, experienced settlers barely survived revealed a downright criminal level of ignorance. At Fort Walsh, Big Bear saw the ravages done to his People by six years of treaty; a century later, Cree historian Blair Stonechild would present the harsh data:

- in 1870 total Indians in treaty areas, estimated 40,000;
- in 1880 total treaty Indians counted, 32,549;
- in 1885 total treaty Indians counted, 20,170.

> "This meant an average of over 2000 more deaths than births each year and a mortality rate of approximately 1 in 10 per year."

Big Bear could not know these staggering numbers, but he breathed them in the air of the tattered camps he visited: Poundmaker, Piapot, Little Pine, Thunderchild, Mosquito, Bear's Head, Red Pheasant, Foremost Man … all friends, some since their childhood … Lucky Man, whose children were his own grandchildren. The endless malnutrition and family deaths, especially of wise Elders and beloved children, of newborns too weak to nurse and mothers too emaciated to have milk and fathers strangling their last dogs to retain every drop of blood—how could that not destroy all will to live? The considered, careful discipline essential in any hunting band, the friendship, the generosity, the mutual help and celebration were annihilated by starvation, by relentless dying. O Great Spirit, how have we lost your incomprehensible gifts so suddenly, so dreadfully? Where has gone the power of life in the land, in the water, the very air we breathe, the sunshine.…

Big Bear's spiritual struggle over the destruction of his world was almost beyond endurance. He could not believe that any but the most hate-filled Whites—the Company men he knew best were as appalled as he—could want human beings to endure what they were now forced into. Clearly the promise they had signed, Treaty Six, and the way it was being applied, must be changed, and he began to dig for what the Whites understood the treaty to say. What it literally said, beyond the often contradictory details he had heard. He tried to talk with every official he could find, with Police Boss Irvine and every Indian sub-agent who dared approach the Cypress Hills, but they were evasively vague with their eternal, slavish response: they obeyed specific orders, they could change nothing. "The Treaty" had become some absolute malevolence hidden beyond reach, and only tiny bits of it could be known, such as "half a pound of flour per grown person every third day," or "no name on Treaty list, no rations."

On May 22, 1882, the *Saskatchewan Herald* editorialized: "Big Bear, with an exceptionally large following of non-treaty and malcontent Indians ... are eking out a miserable existence by fishing [at Cypress Lake] ... It is impossible to over-estimate the danger of having these worthless Indians leading an idle, roaming life, with no higher aim than horsestealing and similar depredations."

"Worthless Indians." In June, translator Peter Erasmus arrived at Walsh, sent by government from Edmonton to convince treaty People to again return north to their reserves. By talking to Erasmus, who understood the treaty disasters as well as any Person, Big Bear found that he could speak to ordinary Whites through their newspapers.

The *Saskatchewan Herald*, August 5, 1882, reported:

> "Though generally not known, it is nevertheless true that the Indians on the plains keep themselves well posted as to what the newspapers say about them.... Big Bear sends a message denying having held secret meetings at which mischief against the whites was discussed.... So far as having held treasonous secret meetings, Big Bear states that repeated efforts were made by Americans and other traders, Louis Riel and others, and Indians from across the line, to commit acts designed to embarrass the Government because the Government had failed to keep its promises to him, but he always resisted their seductions...."

And the Edmonton *Bulletin*, October 21, 1882, stated:

> "A crisis arrived near Cypress last spring, and it is altogether probable that by the [Treaty] Cree being

removed, a first class Indian war was averted.... It was all laid to Big Bear and his band, and he was described as a very bad Indian. Mr Erasmus gives us Big Bear's side of the story, which certainly does not show the southern police or government officials in a very favorable light. In regard to horse stealing, Big Bear said,

'It is true our young men steal, but they were not the first to commence it. Both Blackfoot and Americans were the first to take our horses and continued to do so for two years. When we complained to them here as well as at other places, all the satisfaction we got was that we were told, "Go and do the same." ... I said to them, "Do you want us to break the peace? I thought your office here was of another character, I see plainly you do not want to help us." Our Young Men heard this and this is how so much stealing has been done. We the chiefs try all we can to keep the Young Men from stealing but it is hard to manage them. Having once roused the old spirit, they desire to make braves of themselves and I do not know where or how it will end. There was a time when we had faith in the white man and believed his word … now when a white man says anything to us, we listen, and in the meantime say in our hearts he is lying. How can we have faith in men we know do not take an interest in helping us?… Let an American or any white man say, "There are some of my horses in the Cree camp," the police come at once and all the man has to do is to say "This is my horse" or "that is my horse" and the horse is at once taken and delivered to him without any regard as to where we may have got him from.

'Although we trusted to the law to help us, we never got the benefit of it, because our word is as the wind to the white man.'"

By August 1882, the Canadian Pacific Railway was ripping up the earth past Old Wives Lake and bolting down its double-steel belt for their Iron Horse, as the Sioux called it, to blast across the prairie. Little Pine was not allowed to take his reserve in the Cypress Hills because, despite all treaty declarations of freedom of choice, the government had decided to remove all Indians from near the border by closing Fort Walsh and allowing no reserves south of the railroad. Edgar Dewdney, now Lieutenant-Governor as well as Indian Commissioner, told Big Bear he was building a new headquarters for government where the railroad passed through Where The Bones Lie. Foremost Man, with several dozen followers, disappeared into the eastern Cypress Hills (they would be granted a reserve there thirty-four years later), but the other treaty People around Walsh were forced, by the withholding of rations, to return north for the annuity payments. Nevertheless, Big Bear refused to sign Treaty Six, or to move.

But with bare fishing and nothing to hunt in Canada, unable to cross the border, and receiving no rations, Big Bear's band was dying of malnutrition. Finally his second daughter, who was married to French Eater, broke the band deadlock. Her ten children, Big Bear's grandchildren, were starving, and so were his own children Horsechild and little Earth Woman, and Imasees's two small daughters, and Twin Wolverine's five—what would changing the treaty help if all the children were dead? In October, 133 members of the band, including Big Bear's daughter and Twin Wolverine and Imasees with their immediate families, signed the treaty at Fort Walsh and received signing bonuses and six years' back pay and full rations.

Friday, December 8, 1882. On that day of blowing snow over Fort Walsh, Big Bear gave an incisive four-hour oration explaining how, by lies and deceit and promises never kept, six years of Treaty Six had stolen from his People the Great Spirit's greatest gifts, their independence and their home- land. More support in tools and skill, and above all, more land, was needed for them to live a good and honourable life the way every human being should live in a good and honourable country. But he could refuse no longer. He chose for his councillors Wandering Spirit, Four Sky Thunder, and The Singer. And then, witnessed by Chief Piapot and translator Peter Houri, Indian Agent Allan McDonald and Police Colonel Irvine, Big Bear made his X mark to "transfer, surrender and relinquish ... all his right, title and interest whatsoever ... in and to the territory described in treaty Number Six ... to have and to hold the same unto and for the use of Her Majesty the Queen, her heirs and successors forever."

In so doing, he and the 114 members remaining in his band—including his three wives; his eldest daughter, Nowakich, and her husband, Lone Man, and their five chil- dren; his sons Kingbird and Horsechild; his daughter Earth Woman; and adopted children Small Magpie and Thunder—received treaty annuity back pay and full rations for the winter months. Sir John A. Macdonald's government had won its battle to subjugate the Plains People, even the most independent and self-reliant band of Cree, by a deliberate use of convenient starvation.

And Edgar Dewdney, who had rigidly enforced the hunger policies, congratulated himself on the signing in his 1882 report to the prime minister: "I expect that Big Bear who has, I think, borne unjustly a bad character, will make one of our best chiefs."

CHAPTER EIGHT

One United Land

In the Plains Cree oral tradition, the difficult stories of hunting exile in Montana and the return to the North Saskatchewan under treaty shape-shift into one another. In April 1958, Isabelle Little Bear told her memories to the Bonnyville (Alberta) *Tribune*. She was Imasees's youngest daughter, born in 1873.

> "Prior to Chief Big Bear's last big hunt, our people realized they had lost their land and so they scattered all over like little birds. We who lived under that great Chief Big Bear stayed together and decided to follow the buffalo as far south as we had to go. I don't remember this passage in our history, but have been told very often.... We were not welcome [in Montana]. While waiting to decide what we should do, soldiers arrived with five wagon loads of provisions for us, distributing these supplies amongst our people to make sure we

would be able to reach the Big Line and then be back on Canadian soil. To make sure we did not stop along the way we were escorted by many militaries right up to the Big Line where there was one lonely Red Coat to receive us. The trek back to our former home at Frog Lake [Fort Pitt] was a hard one to live through because of the lack of food and the scarcity of game. We traveled forever northwards and ran into severe storms. Deaths were numerous, we stopped only briefly to bury our dead, amongst the victims of the cold and hunger were my mother and sister. I survived, and was cared for by Mrs. Peter Thunder whom I learned to love as a second mother. My father, Little Bear [Imasees], performed many feats of bravery, which contributed greatly to some of us reaching our destination, Frog Lake."

Big Bear's reunited band did not reach Frog Lake until October 1883; Isabelle's eighty-five-year-old memory has conflated several difficult childhood treks. In spring 1883, the North West Mounted Police moved their post to the railroad at Maple Creek, and in June Big Bear, with five hundred and fifty People, left the Cypress Hills for the last time. They reached Battleford on July 21. A few elderly were transported on ox carts, but most of them walked more than three hundred miles escorted by fifteen Mounted Police and driving a herd of cattle for daily food.

The *Saskatchewan Herald*, August 4, 1883, greeted their arrival with racist venom: "Repatriated pets. The Indian is nothing if not a nuisance. We have Lucky Man and Big Bear with their followers here, and the next thing is to find what to do with them.… On the 22nd the chiefs had a conference with [Indian Agent] Rae.… The situation looks very much like a contest between the good nature of the agent and the gluttony and laziness of the Indians."

When Rae demanded why they refused to go directly to Fort Pitt, where Dewdney had decided they must take their reserve, Big Bear gestured to Poundmaker and his band: "We came here to see our old friends, before they too die of starvation."

Seven years of fighting Treaty Six had curdled his genial wit into gallows humour.

He responded to Anglican priest Thomas Clarke in similar fashion: "You wish to speak to us of the Great Spirit. No, no … at present our ideal religion is flour and pork, pork and flour. Let us discuss nothing more serious. It is the one thing needful today and tomorrow. I am the Black Bear and Black Robe of this band."

Walpole Roland, an itinerant photographer from Port Arthur, comments in his diary:

> "A short, black and shaggy-looking figure clad in a suit of broadcloth [a chief's treaty coat], Balmoral boots, and wearing a large bearskin cap surmounted by three plumes. This is the unwelcome visitor Big Bear, and as his unwieldy body bends backward and forward and his dirty paws dart up and down, while he shows his white teeth to the self-possessed looking Agent, his looks certainly are suggestive of his name; but not withstanding his waving plumes, he does not, when erect, stand more than about four feet four inches, with a chest measurement of perhaps 42 to 48 inches."

In Roland's diary, policemen and Anglicans are invariably "muscular and nearly six feet," and his ludicrous estimate of Big Bear being barely taller than his chest circumference merely underlines his derision. Stony Mountain Penitentiary records list Big Bear's height as five feet, five and a quarter inches, average for Europeans at that time.

With sub-agent Tom Quinn approximately translating, Big Bear and Roland exchanged mockery. When the photographer asked the chief what his picture would cost,

> "His reply almost astounded me, fifty dollars! After giving him some presents I said I could not afford so much … and further that I would try to find if possible a more repulsive looking Indian between here and the Rockies and call him Big Bear. At this he laughed very heartily for a hungry bear, and wishing me good day, gave me a parting shot by adding that I would probably have to go beyond the Rockies to find his rival in ugliness…. He has strongly marked features and is altogether the most obstinate and influential chief in the Northwest."

Little Pine was finally allowed to choose his reserve along the western boundary of Poundmaker's land. Big Bear's many descendants hold to a tradition that he wanted his "land set aside" at Sounding Lake in the shadow of the Neutral Hills but that location, contrary to the treaty, was denied him. He then chose land between the Poundmaker and Strike-Him-On-The-Back/Sweetgrass reserves but, with Thunderchild and Lucky Man just east on the Battle River, that would cluster six influential leaders into one area—and Red Pheasant, Mosquito, Grizzly Bear's Head, and Lean Man were circled in the Eagle Hills barely twenty miles away. Such a Plains Cree landmass near Battleford was too dangerous for "Big Tomorrow" Dewdney. So, as usual, Rae gave Big Bear orders that had no basis in treaty promises: choose your land one hundred and thirty miles upriver, beyond Fort Pitt at Frog Lake; otherwise, you receive no rations.

"Then don't send any police to escort us," growled Big Bear. "My Young Men might be tempted to eat their pretty horses."

The Plains Cree found that Fort Pitt was still the haphazard scatter of buildings it had been when they traded there. Now, as they camped on the surrounding flats, a detachment of Mounted Police arrived to "maintain order" in the area. The twenty-five policemen had only six rideable horses and were commanded by Inspector Francis Dickens (youngest son of novelist Charles Dickens), whose ten-year patronage appointment was one of concentrated ineptitude marked by "recklessness, laziness and heavy drinking." Nevertheless, Dickens did write clear, grammatical reports stating that "everything has, so far, been quiet."

When the Cree received their annual five dollars in October 1883, Big Bear was told to settle on the reserve that

Hayter Reed, Dewdney's assistant, had chosen for them near Frog Lake. Big Bear refused categorically. James Simpson was the Company trader at Frog Lake, which was a strong attraction. But Thomas Quinn was the agent there, a Sioux-Irish half-breed whose aggressive stubbornness the band knew very well because his wife was Lone Man's niece. Also, the Frog Lake farm instructor, John Delaney, had openly lived with a Cree woman after he had had her husband, Sand Fly, falsely jailed for assault and theft. Big Bear and his council wanted none of these problems with government Whites, and no quick encounter with Deputy Minister of Indian Affairs Laurence Vankoughnet would change their minds.

Vankoughnet, the highest Ottawa official Big Bear would ever meet, was a bureaucrat dedicated to his friend Macdonald and to the bottom line of his departmental budget as the Canadian economy slid into recession. He travelled west in 1883 to find how he could cut expenses and, with no grasp of the overwhelming transition from a nomadic hunting to a sedentary reserve life, simply declared that Big Bear's band had already received more than the treaty required. If they did not move onto the reserve by November, all rations—as usual—would be cut off. Then, after a swift tour of several reserves, he disappeared east and slashed the North-West Indian budget by $140,000.

After a summer of struggle at Fort Walsh, the forced treaty signing in winter, and another summer of dry prairie trails and sad visits with many friends, Big Bear knew more than he wanted to know of the desperate misery, the prostrating boredom the Cree endured on their reserves. Life began with food, yes, but true life was more than intermittent doses of lumpy flour and rancid pork, the endlessness of nothing to do. He and his band remained the largest group that had not yet chosen a reserve: that was the one bargaining power they had left to change the treaty. Could they negotiate one large "land set aside" for all Cree—perhaps even for all the Plains People—one huge united land together, straddling rivers and plains and parkland? Could he convince the Blackfoot Confederacy suffering on their reserves, big as they were, to agree? Crowfoot and the Siksika, Red Cloud and the Bloods, Sitting-On-Eagle-Tail-Feathers and the Peigan— was it possible that the land could again feed them as well as it once had, not these endless dry rations.... O Great Spirit, grant wisdom.

And always, the thundercloud on the edge of his thoughts: his last hunt and the vision Coyote had forced him to see beyond the buffalo cow. Bursting out of the ground, spurting between his fingers, blood, uncontrollable—what did it mean?—when would it happen?—must it—why? O Great One, O Only One, have mercy.

Winter was upon them and the men scattered into the forest, trying to rekindle their solitary hunting and trapping skills. But the animals were few, their tracks in the snow largely unreadable memories of their passing. Nevertheless, they worked to be able to support themselves without the tasteless White rations; traders James Simpson and Angus McKay paid them good beef for hauling freight. Big Bear and his sons drove freight sleighs to Edmonton, and visited Chief Pakan in his cabin of logs at Saddle Lake, who reminded them that eight years ago he was already thinking of one huge Cree land along the North Saskatchewan. Yes, Big Bear said, yes, we must talk more of this. All of us, together.

The band lived in unsurveyed boreal forest, their worn hide lodges patched with canvas. There was plenty of wood for fires to keep even the smallest, weakest child warm— better than digging buffalo dung out of drifted snow. But eating squirrels, spruce grouse, and porcupines, chopping down trees for White firewood … it was an inconceivable life for hunter warriors who had once galloped along horizons dancing to the thunder of buffalo. Councillors such as Twin Wolverine, Wandering Spirit, Imasees, and Four Sky Thunder could barely endure it, and those who dreamed of being Worthy Young Men—Kingbird, Round the Sky, Miserable Man, Iron Body, Bad Arrow—found nothing manly in chasing rabbits.

Over and over Big Bear tried to convince his council, and especially his sons, that the only political leverage they had left was their last bit of freedom: to refuse to be fenced in. Use the Queen's law against her, refuse until government agreed to negotiate substantial change, both to the treaties and the little, scattered reserves.

Well, Twin Wolverine said bitterly, if we had our own, particular place, at least we could work for ourselves. Not wear out our horses dragging manure for Whites.

Imasees sneered, You want to dig dirt the rest of your life?

They were clamped tight by iron winter; green spring would certainly come—but with no more great animals. There was only one assured guidance: to dedicate himself to the worship ceremony of a Thirst Dance. Big Bear prayed and meditated and prayed, then, over the winter drifts he sent tobacco to every Plains Cree reserve: Will you come, pray with me in the Thirst Dance? And, together, hold a Grand Council about treaty?

And Poundmaker responded immediately: We will help. Build your Thirst Dance Lodge here beside the Battle River; come, fulfill your vow with us.

The *Saskatchewan Herald*, March 8, 1884, editorialized:

"Big Bear has seen and conversed with many of the chief officers of Indian Affairs, but none of them seems to be 'the head'—there is always some one higher. To settle who this higher power is has now become the one object of his life. To this end he has made up his mind to go to Ottawa, calling at Regina on his way. If there is a head to the Department, he is bound to find him, for he will deal with no one else. If the old growler gets down to Ontario, it is to be hoped he will be kept there."

To meet, to say nothing of speaking with, "the head" of Indian Affairs was impossible for any Indian in 1884. But after years of Morris, Laird, Rae, Crozier, Reed, Irvine, Dewdney, and Vankoughnet, Big Bear understood only too well the endless evasions of government hierarchies; he resolved to "find that one White man than whom there is none higher."

Three months of vigils, prayers, and songs were past, the stories told, the feasts and dancing and offerings made. Cree from Little Pine and Poundmaker and Young Sweetgrass and Lucky Man and Thunderchild had gathered with Big Bear's band. The centre tree had been chosen beside the Battle

River, ceremonially chopped down, and hauled with laughter and singing to the lodge site. There it was raised, its top branches high in the air and its twenty-four rafters radiating out to the surrounding circle of wall. Fresh spring aspen covered the great lodge, a dazzling green plant born suddenly out of the grass above the looping thread of river.

Inside, Big Bear was praying. Carried on the beat of drums, the rhythm of People dancing with him—past the altar, the buffalo skulls, around the Centre Thunderbird Tree hung with offering flags—and sustained by the songs and cries of his gathered community: Grant me wisdom, grant us understanding, we have lost our way of how we should live, grant me my vow, hear our prayer, O Only One, have pity. No eating, no drinking, no sleeping, only movement and petition.

And on the third day the police arrived. At the leafy entrance, Superintendent Crozier in scarlet uniform, two constables, and Louis Laronde, interpreter, who explained that the farm instructor on Little Pine's reserve had been hit with an axe handle by He Speaks Our Tongue when the instructor refused him food; they had come to arrest the Young Man.

Poundmaker and Little Pine stared up at Crozier, whose spirit once went mad on the prairie but who now sat on his horse like polished steel. Warriors muscled together around the chiefs, furious and bristling weapons, while Poundmaker explained that this was their most sacred ceremony. Big Bear was dancing; there would be no arrest near the lodge. And carefully, without anyone raising his voice, they agreed that the ceremony would be completed tomorrow and that the day after, the chiefs would bring Tongue to Crozier. He would be waiting for them at the Poundmaker Agency buildings.

On June 20, 1884, more than three hundred Cree men, some armed and in war paint, others carrying green poplar branches, left the Thirst Dance camps. Big Bear, Little Pine, and Poundmaker walked in the lead, but when they reached the rise overlooking the Agency buildings, the Young Men refused to go farther. Hundreds of women and children watched from the surrounding hills, and together they saw the Uniforms moving into formation. There were at least fifty of them. Ten marched left, ten marched right and hunkered down behind low bastions, rifles poised. Between them the remaining police, mounted and on foot, advanced with arms holstered toward the rise, with Crozier, Laronde, and Farm Instructor Craig walking in the lead. Screams, war whoops, the falsetto ululations of war cries rang over the hills.

Big Bear and Poundmaker advanced to meet Crozier. Poundmaker carried his war club with its four embedded knives, but Big Bear was empty-handed and not wearing his sacred bear paw. The chiefs offered to take the place of the accused—put us on trial in his stead—but Crozier instantly refused. Then Craig recognized He Speaks Our Tongue's face in the crowd, pointed at him and, above all the noise, roared his name. The police surged forward, and Crozier's white gauntlet reached for the Young Man, who cried out, "Don't touch me!"

Laronde shouted Crozier's yell, "I won't touch you! But you must come!"

The hill was a swirl of painted faces and rifles and uniforms and incomprehensible war cries, with Big Bear's poplar leaves waving with many others, and his gigantic voice: "Stop! Wait! Wait!"

And no gun was fired. Like a miracle among the screaming. The cluster of Uniforms was wrestling Tongue down the hill as Cree warriors swirled around them like galloping dervishes, waving their rifles and war clubs and shrieking, but there was no shot. "Wait! Stop!" And in the tangled melee of overwhelming fury He Speaks Our Tongue disappeared behind the bastions, and even as the Cree on foot were charging those flimsy walls, bags of flour and slabs of bacon came flying over. The horsemen wheeled aside in rage, the women and children came running from the hills.

Crozier reported to Dewdney, calmly describing his own adamant courage: "It is yet incomprehensible to me how some one did not fire. Unless we can *keep* the Indians' confidence, there is only one other policy—and that is to fight them."

Big Bear and Little Pine sat together on the hill at Poundmaker's, watching their People swarm the Agency buildings and carry away the food thrown at them.

Little Pine said heavily, All this, for a day's worth of flour.

Imasees galloped below them, waving the revolver he had torn from a policeman's hand but had not fired. Big Bear watched him grow small, vanish where the crest of Cutknife Hill shone in the summer sun—riding out his rage but not his iron anger.

Little Pine said to Big Bear, Your power was strong today. You stopped the blood.

Strong enough to save police. Crozier controls his men, very disciplined.

Yes … but where is our Grand Council?

Ahhhhh.

Vanished in the melee of the arrest of a Young Man, always so hard to control. In the following days they ate fish from the weir they built across the Battle River. The saskatoons were ripening like purple foam in the coulees, and they picked and visited and prepared for travel back to Fort Pitt and the looming necessity of choosing a reserve if they wanted to receive the treaty payments they needed to survive winter. Not live—survive. And while they packed, they heard that Gabriel Dumont had brought Louis Riel from Montana. Riel, who had confronted Canada at Red River and forced Macdonald to establish the province of Manitoba. Riel had already spoken twice to cheering crowds as they neared Batoche:

> "I salute you with all the cheers of my heart, because your different interests are finding the way to the grand union: the grand union of feelings, of views, of endeavors, without which a people can never have any influence, without which a people can never accomplish any thing of importance and without which you could not be happy."

Big Bear was apprehensive about Dumont, Catherine Simpson's brother, who, in a crisis, would not share buffalo with them—and also about Riel's excited musings about war when they met on the Missouri. "Grand Union" was very good, but would a union with Riel be good for Cree? He had done nothing for them in Manitoba fifteen years ago.

On the trail back to Fort Pitt, the band crossed the North Saskatchewan and rested in The Little Hills. While they were remembering Black Powder there, Chief Beardy's messenger found them: "Come for Grand Council to Duck Lake. The Carlton chiefs are here, waiting for you."

And Big Bear recognized that his Thirst Dance vow had been answered, more broadly than he had dared ask.

And so it was that Big Bear's deep, powerful voice filled the August afternoon while the chiefs who had signed Treaty Six at Carlton listened. The emaciated faces of Mista-wasis, Ahtah-kakoop, Beardy, and One Arrow told the miserable story of enduring reserve life for eight years. A police informant who understood Cree jotted down notes:

> "I wish to stay on the land the Great Spirit gave me. I see clearly the one who cheats me. And it is good, in one way, that I am cheated, for now I more fully understand what great good the Only One has given me. I pray and watch for the day when we will, together, speak with one voice.
>
> "What I see is this: I speak for my band as a chief speaks for his People when they are united, but the White agent I speak to isn't like that.

There is always someone higher behind him, whom I never see. I say: Who wastes a bullet on a tail when he knows at another end bear's teeth are waiting? It is time to talk to that one White *than whom there is none higher!* I see my children's bellies hanging slack under their ribs and I say it is time, now!

"Every man of us was blind when making treaty. He did not understand what use he had for it. He was rich, his food and clothing were in his hand; the land was wherever he wanted to go, for we had been given Earth and Buffalo, who needs more to breathe than air? While he was enjoying all this, Government came from far away to this place where we belong and said we must have a treaty. We and the Governor called upon the Great Spirit to witness the treaty, then he invoked the name of the Queen and finally himself. He said, 'We are one blood, I want to help you stand on the same place with my white children, to live together like brothers. We are not going to buy your land. It is a big thing, it is impossible for a man to buy the whole country, we came here to make certain it is kept for you.'

"Therefore, we understand that the land is only borrowed, not bought. And only to the depth a plow can go [six inches], so settlers can grow crops. Anything underground is not given up.

"My friends, I am trying to grasp the promises which they made me. I see my hand closing again and again, but I can find nothing in it. They offered me a spot as a reserve, but since I see that they are not going to be honest, I am afraid to take a reserve. They have given me to choose between several small reserves, but I feel sad to abandon the liberty of my own land when in return I will not get one half of what they have promised me.

"I walk the Earth from the Cypress Hills to Battleford to Pitt, and what I see is the tiny piece of land I am told I must choose and then never leave unless an Agent says I can go. What is that, a mark to see on paper so I can walk on what they borrowed? I belong here! I gaze on our great land, and I feel choked. Is the Queen more to us than Mother Earth? Every man must have the right the Only One gave us: let every man walk where his feet can walk.

"We must stand together with the Only One. Why do we keep turning the same ugly word over and over among ourselves and then swallowing it again? Only a sick dog eats again what he has once vomited out. The white man never hears us speak as one voice, with power. I say, we must choose one of us from all the bands to speak our words. To speak to that White than whom there is none higher, whether that is in Regina or in Ottawa or across the ocean. To speak to the Grandmother like I speak to you. It was done in her name, and I do not believe she wants us to die the way we are.

"It has come to me that we are too scattered. And Pakan at Saddle Lake thinks so too. We are small here, we are smaller there, and who hears us? Who stirs in his sleep when one buffalo runs? But when a herd moves, ahhhhh—we too must shake the ground, we must speak with one thundering voice, we must have one huge 'land set aside' for all of us. Together. Then, when we move, every White will lay his ear to the ground so he won't get trampled.

"It has come to me as through the bushes that you are not united. That you cannot speak for your people because they do not know what can be done. Let us become united and I will speak. Years before the treaty we heard that the Hudson's Bay Company had sold the land to Government. How can you sell land? When, from whom, had the Company ever received it? We know they sold what was not theirs for more money than all our People have received after eight years of treaty, and besides that the Company still has more land than all our reserves together. Now Government says the railroad that strangles the land owns even more than that. While we beg! We sit with salt pork growling in our bellies and talk about how to beg some White to give us another cup of tea. No wonder the buffalo are gone. They would die of shame to be run by hunters whose arms hang slack as pig's fat! Whose councils see no more wisdom blazing before them, whose words are forever complaint and whine!

"I see how government agents bring us everything crooked. They take our lands, they sell them and they buy themselves fine coats, then they clap their hands on their hips and call themselves men. They are not men, They have no honesty. It is then I feel the rope around my neck, and I tell my People I am afraid to take a reserve, to leave my large liberty for such a choked little place where little iron pegs stick in the ground and little agents have nothing to do but watch me try to live. But there is no good in being angry with agents, no one wants blood to stain our land. We want our land clean, pure, so that when we are together on one reserve large enough for our life, together, we will find peace together there. When will you have a big meeting? When will you speak each for your People, this is what we will do, together?"

The chiefs and councillors of the 1,678 People officially listed as alive in the Carlton District sat motionless as rocks, sweat running down their faces. Big Bear spoke softly:

"It sometimes comes to me that we have been breathed over. Like the trance that falls upon us when Windigo is coming. Our power songs call helplessly into the night, our wisdom cries through the trees but we cannot find it. Ice forms in our bodies, we are terrified of the sun rising in another day, eiya, eiy-a-a-a, O Great Spirit, have pity.

"I speak what the Only One gave me to see. Don't allow anyone to poison my words. Speak to your People, and we will altogether make one Grand Council, everyone from the Peace Hills and Edmonton in the west to Piapot in Qu'Appelle, and also Crowfoot on the Bow. I say, we must speak with one thundering voice to that one in government than whom there is none higher!"

The Carlton chiefs did begin speaking with one voice: three days after Big Bear's speech they presented a paper listing eighteen grievances to agent John Macrae. Big Bear told him: "These chiefs should be given what they asked for, all treaty promises must be fulfilled." Macrae promised to send the list to Governor Dewdney—eventually "Old Tomorrow" Macdonald in Ottawa would see it and initiate an investigation—and the chiefs agreed with Big Bear that next year "when the leaves come out" they would gather for a Grand Council of all Treaty Six chiefs, and as many of Treaty Four (Piapot) and Treaty Seven (Crowfoot and Red Crow) as would come. Then, together, they would choose a representative to go speak for them in Regina and Ottawa. Big Bear recommended—perhaps thinking of the Cree sacred number—"The choice of a representative should be given us every four years."

Dewdney knew what Big Bear said; his police had hirelings report on every word the chief uttered. In a twenty-five-page handwritten letter to "My dear Sir John," Dewdney reported on the Duck Lake Council and affirmed: "The Indians ... desire to come to see me in Regina, and you in Ottawa." And in particular, it was Riel's return and the possibility of a Cree-Métis coalition on the Saskatchewan that pushed Macdonald to read the eighteen grievances with great care. And when, upon Riel's invitation, Big Bear met the charismatic Métis, all officials were even more concerned.

Riel welcomed Big Bear in the luxury of a Prince Albert home, with couches and a long table overloaded with food. Riel exclaimed, "Yes, my brother, these are nice things, but if you do as I tell you, you will have grander things, and plenty to eat. I am poor, but you will be rich.... What I say to you I say to all my brother chiefs, and I want you to tell them my words."

Big Bear had eaten in enough claustrophobic houses not to be impressed, but Riel's words made sense. Aggressive White settlers were searching out the best soil along the rivers, and the Métis had no paper title to lands they had lived on for a generation. Always it was land, the Mother Earth. If the Métis made common cause with them in their Grand Council—but Riel and Dumont were such overwhelming leaders, they thought so unlike People. Riel spoke no Cree, he wore a silver cross around his neck, and listened continuously to priests. Could the Great Spirit and Riel's God work together?

Nevertheless, the Cree would convene a Grand Council when the leaves came out, and after that one speaker for all the People would finally face The Highest White Boss. That prospect made Big Bear very happy.

But as his band moved again toward Fort Pitt, Twin Wolverine told him that he and six families were remaining near Battleford; they were considering joining People in the Peace Hills. His thoughtful son, who with him had waved poplar branches during the Poundmaker confrontation, wouldn't wait another year for a reserve. Big Bear told him sadly, I'll send you a message when we decide on the way that is best for us. You are my first son.

CHAPTER NINE

Taking My Name from Me

Inspector Dickens reported to Crozier in October 1884 that Big Bear's five hundred and four band members had fifteen Winchesters and twenty-five smooth-bore muskets.

During the treaty payments at Fort Pitt that month, Big Bear saw a picture of himself for the first time. A glass eye in a box captured on paper black and white shadows of himself and his men without revealing their vivid trading colours. Travelling photographer Cornelius Soule told him that sunlight was the power behind the mystery of his picture. On the right half of it are nine police and Company men; Big Bear stands in the centre beside Bad Arrow, his son Kingbird, and Four Sky Thunder, with Iron Body seated on a buffalo robe in front of them. The Cree are dressed in the ceremonial costumes the Hudson's Bay Company annually gives them to celebrate what is now their 214th year of mutual trade. Big Bear wears a beaver hat decorated with three ostrich plumes, a stripped blanket, and clasps a spray of eagle feathers. Kingbird, also in plumed hat, holds across his body a thick club with a spiralling pattern of spikes sticking out of it.

Despite the celebratory clothes, the Cree are not trading; they are buying what they can with their five-dollar treaty money. And a year from now the Young Men Bad Arrow and Iron Body will stand on a gallows at Battleford with ropes around their necks.

Dickens's report of January 12, 1885, reads: "Big Bear's Indians are working [at Frog Lake], cutting logs and hauling wood for the Indian Department. As long as they work, they will receive rations. All quiet at present."

The settlement at Frog Lake was already much larger than the six Company buildings at Fort Pitt. John Gowanlock was building a grist mill, George Dill a small store, James Simpson ran the Company store and post office, and a Catholic church had been built, in which school was held for whatever children came. Sub-agent Tom Quinn and Farm Instructor John Delaney had the largest houses, and together they controlled the Agency rations. A six-man detachment of police from Fort Pitt maintained White order; they could not, of course, "order" the fact that Delaney's flour ration was thirteen hundred pounds short, nor that the logging the Cree were commanded to do was clearing Quinn's land for better sale to expected settlers.

Isabelle Little Bear was twelve that harsh winter. In 1958 she remembered:

> "As I started attending school taught to us by the resident priest [Father Leon Fafard], I noticed that my people complained all the time while seated around their campfires after sundown. I and the other children played at our games, but could not help hear and see that our friends and neighbors were unhappy, therefore, we felt insecure. Our Chief Big Bear was quite elderly [59] and always tried to tell the other men to wait and be patient, that someday things would be better. The younger men, including my father Little Bear [Imasees], forever bemoaned the fact that we had failed to obtain ourselves a new home amongst the Big Knives [Americans]. These remarks would cause my grandfather to feel very humble because it reflected on his inability to lead his people. It was at this juncture that my father quite unofficially became our leader, although Big Bear was still our chief.

"Around the campfires the conversation centered on the meager rations and how dark the future was. Many times a delegation would go to Mr. Quinn and try to obtain provisions on credit. He always repeated the same words: 'My orders are not to let any provisions out of the agency unless I receive money or trade. Go back home and work.'

"My people are not lazy because I know how hard my foster mother had to work to get enough hides ready for a teepee. It took more than a dozen to make an ordinary sized teepee, and tanning 12 to 17 hides is an awful lot of work. No, our people were not lazy, but we had no ambition to become dirt farmers, nor the habit to go to school and live like the White man. My people have the nature to roam the prairies and follow the buffalo like they did less than 100 years ago. To be told by Quinn to go home and work was like saying, 'Go home and starve.'"

The band men chopped six hundred cords of wood that winter and their families received minimum, increasingly arbitrary, rations. After long council debate, a reserve site was decided upon at Dog Rump Creek, between Frog and

Saddle lakes, though both Imasees and Wandering Spirit opposed the location. The splits about leadership; the growing contempt for Big Bear and his eternal "wait"; the continuous humiliations of having to beg for a relentless diet of bannock and salt bacon; deadly monotony; and a black, helpless future slowly gathered into rage.

Big Bear could not endure the misery and anger. He snow-shoed into the boreal forest with several family members. He followed a deer trail through deep snow and waited where he sensed it would return, leaning between giant aspen whose branches sprayed high over him like prayers spoken into the brilliant air: prayers for understanding, for wisdom, for what more he must know about Whites with all their paper, their slavish impossibilities, their overwhelming weight of more and evermore *things*. And especially for how to negoti-ate one unified land from plain to parkland to this forest— where all People could live together and the Great Earth feed them, hunting or trapping or gardening or farming or ranch-ing as they pleased. Because here they belonged!

He found muskrat dens in a creek bank, trapped the animals, and stripped off their fur the way Black Powder had taught him, a boyhood memory that shimmered like the aroma of buffalo hissing fat into festival fire. And beaver. He found two lodges; carefully dug snares through the ice into their runways; and caught half of every lodge, including two huge bucks, and dragged them back to camp, to the delight of Sayos and the others. They scraped and stretched the pelts, ate every bit of meat and organs and tail, and Horsechild smeared himself with castoreum and pranced around the lodge smelling so smoke-musky beaver that they finally tossed him out, laughing, to wash himself in snow. And at night there were winter stories:

> "Once, long ago when animals talked like People, a man and woman had an only son. It seems they dearly loved him and took good care of him, but one day, when they were working outside, they lost their child. They were very sad, and did not know the child was really alive, and it appears it had been taken by a bear. The bear took care of the child all summer, and winter too, and as often as the man performed his worship, the bear knew it at once. He knew every time the pipe was filled. And this is what he must always have said to the child: 'Grandchild, again I am being invited,' he must have said. And then, finally...."

Henry Halpin, a young trader at Cold Lake who spoke fluent Cree, was listening. He was travelling to Frog Lake for supplies and had been invited to sleep in Big Bear's lodge. On March 19, while returning to Cold Lake, he stopped at the chief's camp for tea and told him, as he later testified under oath, that he had "read in the Saskatchewan *Herald* that Riel had stopped the mails at Batoche." The chief was "very surprised" and had said "I think it is very strange." But despite this troubling news, Big Bear did not return to Frog Lake. He hunted moose and visited Halpin at Cold Lake: "He came to my house before dinner on the 21st and went away on the evening of the 22nd," and his small party did not return to Frog Lake until April 1.

And they instantly heard the astounding news, which Imasees had discovered in a warning letter from Dickens that he stole off Quinn's desk and had a local Métis read to him: On March 26, the Batoche Métis under Dumont and Riel had fought a battle with Crozier at Duck Lake. Four Métis and one Cree were shot, two police and ten other Whites. Crozier and his men then retreated to Prince Albert. And Fort Carlton, with all its Company and police supplies, had been burned to rubble.

This was electrifying for the Cree Young Men: Crozier's police killed and in retreat! But, strangely, Quinn had decided that everything was quiet and had ordered the six local police back to Fort Pitt, since "their presence in Frog Lake only tended to exasperate the Indians." Big Bear knew the situation to be utterly different, and he sent his caller through the camp calling for a council. But Wandering Spirit refused to attend— a sure sign that the war chief was preparing for confrontation. A Cree head chief has no authority beyond what his People willingly, freely grant him, and Big Bear now faced the ominous reality of being ignored by his councillors. Surprisingly, Imasees agreed to go with him to Quinn, and he listened silently while Big Bear assured the agent, as interpreter John Pritchard later testified, that "he [Big Bear] was not going to rise to war, he was going to be loyal. He wanted to show the Government, he said, that he did not want to do anything at all."

But even as Big Bear repeated these words in total sincerity, he recognized on his son's clenched, winter-hardened face that the situation in Frog Lake was no longer dangerous: it was deadly.

That evening Wandering Spirit moved his lodge closer to the lake, and through the night most of the band followed him. In 1982, Jimmy Chief told the story of how his grandfather Little Bear and Wandering Spirit

"… started to build a place [beside Frog Lake] for a war dance, and when it was finished they started to dance. While the dance was going on Wandering

Spirit got up and said, 'Quiet! Tomorrow I am going to eat two-legged meat! So what do you think?' No one answered him and pretty soon they started dancing again. Then Wandering Spirit stopped the dance again. 'Hey, listen,' he called out. 'Tomorrow if you don't want to join me, then go home and put on your wives' dresses!' So they started to agree, 'Okay, okay.' They started to dance again until it was almost daylight. Then Wandering Spirit stopped the dance again. 'Look here,' he laughed at the ones who were leaving, 'I just made some of our brothers like women!'"

Before dawn on April 2, 1885, the warriors in war paint led by Imasees were in Frog Lake settlement. When Big Bear arrived, some were breaking into the Company store. Unfortunately, highly respected James Simpson had gone to Fort Pitt, and only his terrified young clerk, William Cameron, still in night clothes, was behind the counter. Miserable Man was about to leap over the counter when Big Bear, in the doorway, shouted, "Stop! Don't touch anything! If you want something, ask Cameron and he'll write it down." The Young Men could not yet disobey him to his face; they left with what they had already taken.

Big Bear knew that as soon as he left, the men would return to the store for the ammunition and powder. They were everywhere now, stripped to breechcloths in the cold air and painted. His men, who had followed him all their lives, would not look at him: they stood with guns raised around Quinn's and Pritchard's and Delaney's houses—obviously the agent and his wife and nephew, Henry Quinn, and Delaney and his wife and the mill builder John Gilchrist and his wife were already captives. Big Bear could only watch as Imasees and twenty warriors brought the other Whites together: William Gilchrist, John Williscraft, trader George Dill, carpenter Charles Gouin, and three Métis men visiting him. Then the church bell began to ring. Wandering Spirit emerged from Pritchard's house with Quinn and his Cree wife; the Delaneys and Gilchrists appeared on their doorstep as well. The war chief waved his rifle and, with some forty warriors circling around, herded the Whites down the short trail into the church.

When Big Bear entered the church, he could not know that Fathers Fafard and Marchand were trying to celebrate Maundy Thursday Mass, the commemoration of Jesus' betrayal. He smelled incense, heard the priests chanting, sounds swinging back and forth around the low altar. As the

Whites and a few Cree knelt in the pews to pray, Wandering Spirit entered. As Cameron wrote:

> "He moved cat-like on his moccasined feet to the centre of the church and dropped on his right knee, his Winchester clutched in his right hand, the butt resting on the floor. His lynx-skin war-bonnet, from which depended five large eagle plumes, crowned his head; his eyes burned and his hideously painted face was set in lines of deadly menace ... while he half knelt, glaring up at the altar and the white-robed priests."

The mass ended abruptly when the war chief stood erect and shouted, "That's enough!" He ordered both priests to remove their vestments and told the Métis altar boy, Salamon Pritchard: "You too, hang up those things!" As the frightened congregation with the priests filed past him, Big Bear was concentrating on keeping them safe: if they submitted quietly to being captives while the stores were raided and horses were taken and government cattle were shot for butchering—and especially if Tom Quinn could keep his vicious mouth shut—there was still hope. But several men were weaving about from more than sheer excitement, almost as if they were drunk. Had they found liquor or the alcoholic painkiller medicine at the Company or Dill's store, perhaps even the altar wine the priests hid in the church? Big Bear could only watch; Wandering Spirit with his Winchester was in command.

As the crowd moved up the road toward Pritchard's and Delaney's houses, Catherine Simpson stood in her doorway watching it pass. Big Bear leaned in exhaustion against the doorpost.

Mrs. Simpson was frightened. If only her man were there!

Big Bear said, "Yes ... but don't be afraid. Better gather up your things, I think there is going to be trouble. I can't be everywhere to look over my young men."

And as a nervous Catherine Simpson later testified at Big Bear's trial, "Pritchard and Tom Quinn came into my house. Tom Quinn said this: Big Bear, could I remain at my own house, and Pritchard the same? Oh I suppose you could, Big Bear said.... While Big Bear was eating, I was packing up my little things. I heard a shot outside and I ran out to the door and I saw the man [Tom Quinn] fall, so I went back into my house again. Big Bear got up and went out and I heard him say, 'Don't do so, stopping it ... leave it alone!'"

But on April 2, 1885, there were no leafy poplar branches to wave, and Big Bear's enormous voice roaring "Stop! Stop!"

was lost among gunshots, screams, war cries, whoops, cheers, shrieks. As Big Bear's granddaughter Isabelle would remember:

> "Some young men were daring each other … it all happened so quickly I cannot say for sure what happened other than we saw Wandering Spirit raise the gun and fire at the Agent … Mr. Quinn, who was wearing a Scottish beret, suddenly fell forward and his cap tumbled to within a few feet from where I stood. Immediately Wandering Spirit and his friend yelled, 'Let's all go and get some [two-legged meat] to eat now.' All I remember is that I was then very frightened and ran away…."

Tom Quinn sprawled in blood before Pritchard's house, and the other Whites made the mistake of running: the warriors were after them, whooping in frenzy, some sprinting, some on horseback running the terrified Whites down like buffalo.

Big Bear could only stand, frozen, and watch his hopes and plans and unending prayers for a better treaty and one huge Plains People Confederation disintegrate in the spring air. All the White men living at Frog Lake except for three were killed: Tom Quinn first and then Charles Gouin were shot dead in front of Pritchard's house. John Delaney, John Gowanlock, Father Leon Fafard, and Father Felix Marchand were shot dead on the trail leading north to the lake. John Williscraft, George Dill, and twenty-year-old William Gilchrist, who ran best of all, were chased down on horseback and shot dead along the same trail.

But the two White women, Teresa Delaney and Teresa Gowanlock, were not shot; they were torn from their husbands' bodies and taken captive.

Company clerk William Cameron was first hidden under a clothes pile by Catherine Simpson, then she led him away disguised under a red blanket like a Cree woman.

Henry Quinn, Quinn's young nephew, escaped between the buildings and reached Fort Pitt on April 3, Good Friday, with news of the killings.

Toward evening the third Frog Lake White man to survive returned from Fort Pitt in his buckboard. James Simpson found the settlement deserted, the church, the houses, the barns abandoned, doors and windows smashed, all plundered. Quinn's mutilated body lay in front of Pritchard's house, Charlie Gouin's nearby. After looking into his destroyed store, Simpson drove to the Cree camp where, as he later testified at Big Bear's trial, he found his old friend of forty years with "all the Indians sitting in a circle. I asked him, hallo, I said, you are here ... did you make a good hunt? He said, no, and that is all I asked him just then, and then he said to me afterwards, if you wish to come into my tent and remain in my tent, you [can] come in.... [But] I went down to my own tent first [to his wife and stepson, Louis Patenaude] and then about an hour or so after I went back to Big Bear's tent, and I said to him, I am sorry to see what you have done here. Well, he says, it is not my doings. I said, now this affair will all be in your name, not your young men. It will be all on you, carried on your back. He says, it is not my doings, and the young men won't listen, and I am very sorry for what has been done.... They have been always trying to take my name from me. I have always tried to stop the young men, and they have done it this time and taken my name away from me."

CHAPTER TEN

The Wild Young Men

"It will be all on you, carried on your back."

On April 4, 1885, news of the Frog Lake killings reached the rest of Canada by telegraph from Battleford. The media understood nothing about Wandering Spirit or Imasees or Cree Young Men. All they knew about was the "cowardly, very troublesome" Chief Big Bear, and instantly he became a "bloodthirsty savage," a "fiend to be wiped out of existence." In particular, hysteria about the two White women known to have survived, their certain, frightful abuse and "fate worse than death" at the hands of savages, drove thousands of Canadian men to volunteer for the army that "Old Tomorrow" Macdonald was assembling with astounding speed. Conquer the West, finish the Indians and Métis!

As news of Crozier's rout by Dumont at Duck Lake burned across the west, a few starving Cree pillaged stores at Peace Hills, Green Lake, Lac la Biche, Beaver Lake, and Cold Lake; Poundmaker's band ransacked some Battleford stores after the villagers fled to the police stockade and Agent

Rae refused to talk with them. An Assiniboine in the Eagle Hills killed a despised farm instructor, and another a hated settler.

But there was no general Cree uprising; along the Saskatchewan, no band travelled to Batoche to assist the Métis. At Frog Lake, the war council debated whether to shoot the remaining Whites and local Métis who worked for the government as translators and contractors. The neighbouring Woods Cree bands joined them for days of feasting on plunder and butchered cattle, but they strongly opposed more killing. Catherine Simpson and John Pritchard were related to Chief Cut Arm's band; they and the Woods Cree protected the captives in their lodges, especially the two Teresas, who were never physically hurt but cared for as well as the chaotic circumstances allowed. And though Imasees and Wandering Spirit, always with his rifle in his hand, dominated the combined council decisions as their continuing rage against everything White moved them, no one else was shot. Big Bear said nothing in council.

Ten days of feasting, wild dance, song, war exploits retold, cattle run like buffalo, and endless councils. For Fort Pitt must be next: four buildings piled to their peaked roofs with Big Boss McLean's magnificent Company stores, and in two other buildings scrawny Inspector Dickens with his twenty-four police and all of six horses! Wandering Spirit had more than three hundred mounted warriors: what he needed was Winchesters and ammunition.

When Henry Quinn arrived at Fort Pitt with his horrifying news, McLean and Dickens prepared for an attack. Fort Pitt now stood without palisade on the flats beside the North Saskatchewan River, so all they could do was knock down outbuildings, barricade the spaces between larger buildings with logs and grain sacks, and cut rifle-holes between the house logs. And wait. The aspen and willows burst green along the river in beautiful stillness. Finally Dickens, against McLean's strongest warnings, sent out a patrol. His three men had barely disappeared when armed warriors appeared above the fort. To quote Dickens's laconic diary:

> "Monday, April 13 [actually Tuesday, April 14]. Fine weather. Const. Loasby, Cowan and Henry Quinn left for a scouting expedition to Frog Lake. A number of Indians arrived from Frog Lake, at top of hill 800 yards behind Fort. Sent letter signed by Big Bear demanding that police lay down their arms and leave the place, they report all prisoners safe.... Mr. McLean went out and parleyed with them and gave them grub. By contents of letter

it appears 250 armed men are around the Fort to our 38, plus the three Misses McLean. Everything quiet during night."

John Pritchard later testified that Big Bear persuaded Imasees and Wandering Spirit not to attack Fort Pitt immediately but to urge McLean to surrender. So next morning McLean again walked with his interpreter, Francois Dufresne, to the camp just beyond the horizon hills. Big Bear passed the council pipe around but did not speak. The war chief argued that the Cree wanted to get rid of government completely and live only with the Hudson's Bay Company "as they and their forefathers before them had, while receiving many useful supplies and help." As McLean remembered it:

"When Wandering Spirit approached me, he put some additional cartridges into his Winchester and then, placing it in readiness on his arm, he put his hand on my shoulder and said, 'Do not speak too much. That is why I killed the Agent. You say too much about Government, we are tired of him and all his people and we are now going to drive them out of our country. Why do you keep Government's few Red Coats in your Fort? That is the only thing we have against you. That Fort was built for us many years ago, and we would have killed them long ago were it not for you and your family being in there.'"

McLean could not convince Wandering Spirit that the twenty-five "Red Coats" meant that Government (the war chief spoke of it as a person) could send thousands of soldiers armed with cannons to enforce the Queen's law. While they were tussling over these ideas, disaster struck: the three returning police scouts blundered into the camp and the warriors' tension burst into action. To quote Dickens:

"[April 15]: During parley the three scouts out yesterday galloped through the camp towards Pitt. Const. Cowan was shot dead and Loasby wounded in two places before hauled over barrier. Horse killed and Quinn got away, but missing. Indians fired upon by all. McLean and Dufresne taken prisoner. Indians threatened to burn Fort tonight with coal oil brought from Frog Lake."

The barricaded buildings could not withstand an attack by fire. McLean wrote his wife a note explaining that, to prevent more bloodshed, the civilians must surrender to the Cree and the police must use the Company scow and leave, downriver for Battleford. Big Bear persuaded the warriors to give the police some hours to get ready (they used the time to pack, scatter gunpowder, and smash extra rifles) and himself dictated a letter to Henry Halpin for Sergeant Martin, Dickens's second in command:

"My dear friend:

"Since I have met you long ago we have always been good friends, and you have from time to time given me things, and that is the reason I want to speak kindly to you; so please try and get off from Pitt as soon as you can. And tell your Captain that I remember him well, for since the Canadian Government had left me to starve in this country, he sometimes gave me food, and I don't forget the blankets he gave me, and that is the reason I want you all to get off without bloodshed.

"We have had a talk, I and my men, before we left our camp, and we thought the way we are doing now the best—that is, to let you off if you would go. So try and get away before the afternoon, as the young men are wild and hard to keep in hand.

—Big Bear

"P.S. You asked me to keep the men in camp last night, and I did so; so I want you to go off today.
—Big Bear."

Snow began to fall as the wounded Constable Loasby was carried down the bank of the North Saskatchewan and into the scow. Then the twenty-three police clambered in and pushed into the crushing river ice. They left Cowan's mutilated body on the flats, and forty-four civilians to trudge into the hills as captives. Individual Cree families volunteered to take the captives in, guard, and care for them. Eleven McLeans surrendered, nine of them children, including the three eldest—Elizabeth, Amelia, and Kitty—who spoke fluent Cree and had stood guard for two weeks, fired guns during the scout disaster, and fearlessly carried messages between Whites and Cree.

Dickens's siege diary ends: "Wednesday, April 15 [Thursday, April 16]: Very cold weather. Travelled."

Despite churning ice and a blizzard, the police reached Battleford safely. Dickens's official report offered no alternatives to the fact that McLean's trust in Big Bear's word saved both civilians and police from annihilation. Rather, he tried to cover his leaving civilians in the hands of hostiles with this final, self-righteous sentence: "The surrender of the civilians was entirely owing to the pusillanimity of Mr. McLean of the Hudson's Bay Company."

During three days of winter the Cree war party feasted, plundering Fort Pitt, but when the sun returned they travelled back to their families on the shore of Frog Lake with captives and booty. The settlement stores, houses, and church had been burned, most of the bodies buried, but Quinn's lay rotting beside the puddle where it fell. For a month, while spring gathered, they lived well and held councils to consider what was to be done. Wandering Spirit sent messages to numerous reserves, but, as John Pritchard later testified, every chief, including Pakan, refused "to come in and join them."

Meanwhile, the government inevitabilities moved on with deliberate speed, as Big Bear knew they would. During April soldiers by the thousands arrived on the railroad and marched north in three columns hauling cannons, field artillery, and massive supplies: General Middleton left from Fort Qu'Appelle with the main militia destined for Batoche, Colonel Otter from Swift Current for beleaguered Battleford, and Major General Strange from Calgary to Edmonton, determined to reach Fort Pitt. On April 24, Dumont and his Métis fought Middleton to a standstill at Fish Creek; on May 2, Otter's attack on Poundmaker's sleeping camp at Cutknife Hill was beaten into desperate retreat by the brilliant tactics of warriors under war chief

Fine Day. Two days later Wandering Spirit received a letter from Poundmaker's band written in French promising the Cree generous supplies if they came to help "take Battleford and then go on and join Riel at Batoche." Big Bear said he would not go, and after two days of fierce disagreement between Plains and Woods Cree, Imasees himself rode for Poundmaker's to verify the situation. In the meantime, Wandering Spirit began moving the fifteen hundred People toward Fort Pitt, the first leg of a very long possible journey to Poundmaker's and eventually Batoche.

News came from Pakan at Saddle Lake that an army had reached Edmonton. Wandering Spirit was convinced they were the "thousands of American soldiers" Riel had assured him last summer would march in from Montana to kill Government and offer the Cree a splendid new treaty. But Imasees returned with news that government troops were everywhere, in overwhelming numbers. Poundmaker had driven Otter's soldiers off, but after Fish Creek, Middleton continued his advance on Batoche. And the troops in Edmonton were not Americans; they were Canadian soldiers heading for Fort Pitt.

Imasees had not heard, and so no one in camp could know, that on May 12, Middleton's troops had overrun Batoche—thirteen Métis, eleven Canadians killed—and ended the rebellion with Riel's surrender. Gabriel Dumont had vanished into the prairie.

But Big Bear recognized clearly what he most feared. The fountain of blood had burst up with nine men killed at Frog Lake. He had almost managed to squash it at Fort Pitt—only one man killed by blunder—but it would surely flow again, and inevitably now among his own People, because they were led by men who hated Whites. Here in Canada no police had ever killed a single Person, yet Wandering Spirit and Imasees and Lucky Man longed for the American Long Knives, who they knew had often attacked and killed sleeping Indian camps. And even if the Cree, now, had thousands of warriors, where could they get enough guns and ammunition to kill any Whites? Only from Whites! Why could he no longer convince his own son that talk was the only power People had? Words, only words.

With words he had saved sixty-eight lives at Fort Pitt, so he would speak once more in council. As McLean recalled Big Bear's words:

> "You have heard the news from Poundmaker. It is alarming to you, what are you going to do about it? You were in a hurry to commence trouble, and

now you have it, the soldiers of the Queen have come to fight you, and very shortly you will likely have to show how you can fight them. You were told that they do not take their women and children with them when they go out to fight, and you will see it now."

Big Bear's great council voice would not speak again. Imasees and Wandering Spirit as war chiefs now led all the Cree, including the intimidated Woods Cree.

At Fort Pitt they dug out the last Company flour and rounded up straying cattle. Then, while the buildings burned, they trailed east paralleling the river cliffs, meandering toward Battleford. Mounted scouts guided the long, straggling trek of ox- and horse-drawn carts, burdened women and children trudging with men herding cattle, horses and dogs dragging travois, captives bent under bedding. At the very end, Big Bear walked with his youngest children; he carried a food pack and his sacred bundle.

They could advance only a few miles a day through the boreal landscape, crossing muskegs and streams running with melt water. Beneath the high crest of Frenchman Butte the leaders decided to rest and hold a Thirst Dance to revive everyone's spirits. No preparation ceremonies had been held, but the centre tree was set and the leafy lodge almost complete when a scout galloped down from the Butte. Using a spyglass taken at Fort Pitt, he had seen canoes and six scows crowded with men and horses rounding the bend of the North Saskatchewan River above Pitt!

Ceremony dissolved into a flurry of retreat. Wandering Spirit ordered the camp moved from the indefensible clearing to beyond a wooded hill north of the Butte. Scouts rode out to establish the soldiers' positions and discovered Inspector Sam Steele's Scouts tracking their trail from Fort Pitt. Shots exploded in the spring dusk, and the warrior Maymenook was hit. Corporal Thomas McClelland threw a rope around Maymenook's neck and dragged the body in triumphant circles, galloping up a hill. Someone slashed the rope, and they left the warrior's body to rot.

General Strange's two hundred infantry, thirty cavalry, and one nine-pounder gun glimpsed Wandering Spirit's muzzle-loader and Winchester-armed warriors at sunrise on May 28, two miles north of Frenchman Butte. The Dominion Survey later proved that the battleground fit exactly into the never cultivated northeast quarter of Section 35, Township 53, Range 25, west of the third meridian. Trooper Joseph Hicks recorded:

> "We had advanced perhaps three miles when the Indians opened fire on our advance guard.

"The Indians had chosen an impregnable position.... On the north side of a muskeg was a small hill or rising ground in big timber right down to near the water. On this [hill] they had dug trenches about four feet deep and had logs placed so that they could fire from under the logs without exposing themselves to our fire. The approach to this position was exposed to a direct fire from the trenches ... at least a quarter of a mile long.... The 65th Battalion extended to the muskeg's edge, indeed a number of them went in up to their necks only to find that they could not even swim because of the tall grass. They then lay down and fired at the trenches, which was all that could be done."

Big Bear was well behind those expert trenches, with the women and children and captives down in wooded ravines. When Strange's first nine-pounder cannon ball tore through the aspen overhead, the huddled camp broke into chaos. Big Bear organized the retreat, assuring the terrified People that the gun was aimed too high to be dangerous. Half their carts and animals were left behind in the flight. The cannon continued firing, and they heard explosions behind them— that big gun speaks twice, he explained, once when it fires and again when the ball lands and explodes. They heard the trees shudder even when they were several miles away.

Big Bear had helped dig the trenches overlooking the bare glacis. He knew the warriors would stop the soldiers there because Wandering Spirit could choose and build a defensive position as brilliantly as he could make a thousand People vanish before the American Army. At war tactics he was superb. But seemingly he could not grasp the strategies of politics, the agreements that words alone can fashion; that People cannot long be led with only a loaded Winchester in your hand.

The distant gun stopped soon after the first warriors left the trenches and caught up with the fleeing camp. The men said the gun had finally gotten range of their trenches with those exploding balls. Five warriors were wounded and another, He Speaks Our Tongue, was dying with his leg blown away. By then the soldiers and gun had retreated as well, so they had time for Tongue's harrowing death chant and burial. Elizabeth McLean would remember that, during the mourning, she first noticed that Wandering Spirit's hair was turning white. Pritchard and five half-breed families, together with the two Teresas, had disappeared during the battle. Some men rode back for supplies scattered in flight, and then, while other warriors fought skirmishes with soldier scouts, for the next four days Wandering Spirit led the People north. Over hills, through intermittent rain and dense forest, a remarkable retreat into wilderness. Cameron, Halpin, and other captives were let go, but the main camp with the McLeans and Simpsons struggled on until one brilliant evening they reached Loon Lake Crossing. Facing the lake, arms high, Big Bear gave thanks for one more day, for the lovely call of the loons across the light on the water that warmed dryness into their sodden clothing.

He found Simpson beside his small fire. They had not talked since Fort Pitt burned, merely plodded on day after day wherever Wandering Spirit led. Simpson was scraping mud from his moccasins and protruding toes.

Big Bear said quietly, Where have gone your horses? Your beautiful horses?

They always hated bush, mud, Simpson muttered. He glanced up. Wandering Spirit sat staring into his fire, his small daughter folded in his arms. Simpson said, He talks with Mrs. McLean. McLean told me he asked her, What would your God do to someone who did what I've done?

What did she say?

The Good Book says a man is punished for his evil.

Big Bear said bitterly, Your God has so much practice, punishing.

It was murder.

Quinn said "No!" to the war chief four times.

Yes.

It almost seemed they could be friends again. Simpson asked, Why don't your men let us go? The soldiers will never stop while we're captive.

The men think, once you're gone, nothing would stop the soldiers from killing us all.

But McLean is a powerful White. If he was free, he could maybe persuade the soldiers to stop shooting.

I know, Big Bear said, maybe. But it has, I think, gone too far.

That was the last time they talked. Before dawn Sam Steele's Police Scout Cavalry emerged under the trees and attacked. The sleeping camp burst into defence and flight, Woods Cree Chief Cut Arm was shot dead as he darted from his lodge. There were captives everywhere, but Steele's men fired indiscriminately; two shots whistled past Kitty McLean wading with a child through the crossing. In 1975, Horsechild's wife, Mary PeeMee, told the Cree story of June 3, 1885, the last military battle fought in Canada:

"At Loon Lake the soldiers caught up with them. The people were all afraid, but Big Bear's medicine was so strong, he would always be safe. Around his neck he wore a necklace of beads. A bear's claw rested in the hollow of his throat. As long as he wore that claw there, nothing could hurt him. Big Bear walked out into the open while his people fled. It was as if he placed an invisible wall between his people and the soldiers. The soldiers could not see him either. When his people were far enough away to be safe again, he caught up with them."

"Safe" for the Cree could only mean north, farther into the maze of muskegs, lakes, forest, stony hills, creeks. But not before they buried the five warriors shot at Loon Lake and aged Sitting-At-The-Door, who, in terror, had hanged herself. The fleeing Cree heard that two huge riverboats full of soldiers had arrived at Fort Pitt from Battleford, that whole battalions were searching for them from three directions. They knew a thousand People could not continue in flight together, and small groups broke away, trekking toward Fort Pitt to surrender. Woods Cree with the McLeans and Simpsons disappeared across the Beaver River, and when Wandering Spirit pursued them, the pursuers joined the pursued. Together they struggled through boreal wilderness and reached Fort Pitt on June 22 to jubilation in the enormous soldier encampment. The Cameron and

Pritchard parties had already arrived. The Woods Cree surrendered, as did Wandering Spirit, who had started the Cree's eighty-two-day triumph and travail by killing Tom Quinn on April 2.

Big Bear was not puzzled that Wandering Spirit surrendered or surprised that, when taken prisoner, the war chief tried to kill himself with a knife. There had always been a split in Wandering Spirit, a chasm between gentleness and furious pride, between a rage at humiliation and the shame of guilt. Now the White doctors forced him to stay alive until a rope could be cinched around his neck.

There were only a few hundred Plains Cree left free, moving through swampy forest with noisy soldiers blundering about and finding no one. Their supplies were finished, and several leading men decided that only the prairie could save them. While more groups trickled away to surrender at Turtle Lake and Battleford, Big Bear's sons Imasees and Kingbird, together with Lucky Man, all implicated in the Frog Lake killings, led a hundred People between Canadian patrols on a six-hundred-mile flight south into Montana. As some Onion Lake Cree would remember it, "Imasees commandeered the best horses and many needed supplies and left his tribal kinsmen as a traitor might leave his comrade. [He] left behind disgust and ill will among those who wanted to join the exodus but were deserted by Imasees."

The United States held no promise for Big Bear. He mourned his sons who had fled—and Twin Wolverine, who with the Peace Hills bands had remained clear of the conflict—none of whom he would ever meet again. But a few People were still left, including his wife and Horsechild, and so he could not remain in the forest, much as he loved it even without a horse. A soldier camp at Turtle Lake and continuous patrols from Battleford made Jackfish Lake and The Little Hills impossible. But there was Fort Carlton, where his mother and father took him as a little boy, where he first met good Whites who laughed and danced, drank tea and traded honestly, helped you live as free as you pleased, with fine steel needles and axes that never burst in the cold. Carlton was burned rubble, they said; perhaps no soldiers would be there.

They easily avoided Otter's troops at Turtle Lake and reached the North Saskatchewan River starving. They hid when a steamboat filled with soldiers paddle-wheeled past, the smell of frying meat so good they almost fainted. Then they built rafts, crossed the river, and Big Bear's wife, with the other women and children, trudged on to find shelter with the Duck Lake bands. But twelve-year-old Horsechild refused to leave his father. They were almost at Carlton when they stopped at a trader's tent for food. The man gave them hardtack to gnaw but slipped away to report them. And so, on July 2, 1885, Big Bear surrendered, as the press commented sarcastically, to the only four policemen in the North-West who were not hunting him.

CHAPTER ELEVEN

A Recommendation to Mercy

Profusely, often wildly, illustrated weekly papers were published in eastern Canada throughout the brief North-West Rebellion, and by June the front pages of dailies were dominated by the hunt for the one remaining "savage," Big Bear. When the "Big Bear captives" straggled into Fort Pitt, telegraph accounts from reporters on the spot were columns wide, especially stories of the two widows and the McLean family with their nine children, including Ewan, a "fat, chubby little fellow not two years of age." To every newspaper's amazement, "Not one of [the captives] had been subjected to bodily injury or ill-treatment of any sort." Consequently, after news of Big Bear's surrender came—"a sixty-year-old coward, a black Indian with an enormous head"—all press interest in Big Bear ceased. What Sir John A. Macdonald called "the five million dollar unpleasantness," "a mere domestic trouble," which had killed a mere eighteen

Indian, nineteen Métis, and sixty White soldiers and civilians, was ended. Except for the trials and the executions.

Taken to Prince Albert, Big Bear again saw himself in a photograph: seated, alone, a red-striped white Company blanket draped over his shoulders and heavy hair to reveal only his gaunt face and roped, bare feet. His eyes tight as slits stare straight into the camera; looking at the world has exhausted him.

By July 15, Big Bear, Horsechild, and other prisoners had been hauled to Regina for trial. As Horsechild's wife Mary told it:

> "The wagons that took them carried much food. My man said after each meal enough was thrown away to feed all the people for many days. Big Bear hurt to see it wasted when he knew our people had nothing.… Big Bear could have escaped, you know. There were no handcuffs or jails that could have kept him locked up. They say he used to take his handcuffs off and play with them. He could walk in and out of the jail cell."

In 1983, Alphonse Little Poplar continued that story of Big Bear's power. One day, depressed by being forever sealed behind walls, he walked out of his locked cell in the police prison to sit in the yard sunshine. Soon frantic guards came running, so he went back in.

> "When they entered the building, for a moment no one saw Big Bear. The next they saw of him, he was standing inside his cell. He asked the interpreter to come over. 'Tell [them] … I am very sorry that I frightened them and I will not do it again. You may also remind them that when the Great Spirit gave us sunshine and fresh air, he intended that it was for all to enjoy.'"

For more than a century most Canadians have believed that the North-West Rebellion was a Métis-Indian uprising. The fact is that, except for individual Natives, not a single treaty band joined Riel. The two traditional chiefs who went to Batoche with a few men, the Cree One Arrow and the Sioux Whitecap, did so because the Métis coerced them. Poundmaker's hungry men looted deserted Battleford only after Indian Agent John Rae refused to so much as talk to them, and they later fought no more than necessary to repel Otter's attack on their sleeping band at Cutknife Hill. In 1984, John Tootoosis, Elder on the Poundmaker Reserve, interpreted 1885 this way:

"When the Metis people were preparing to have this uprising, the Indian people said no. We won't support you. We signed an agreement with the Crown not to fight any more; they were to live at peace with these people. We signed a treaty [Cree, *âsotamâkêwin*, "a promise"], we have to live up to this treaty."

Nevertheless, by August 1885, there were as many Cree as Métis in prisons at Battleford and Regina. Gabriel Dumont, who had organized the Métis army and personally shot more Canadian soldiers than anyone, was safe in the United States, but the trial of Louis Riel—who had shot no one but was nonetheless charged with levying treasonous war—began on July 20. By July 31, Riel had destroyed his lawyer-imposed defence of insanity by making a brilliant, reasoned statement of his behaviour to the court. The jury found him guilty and Judge Hugh Richardson sentenced him to hang.

On August 13, the elderly One Arrow from Duck Lake was the first Cree chief to stand trial. He was charged with treason-felony: of intending to levy war against the Queen, her Crown, and Dignity. Peter Houri, one of the most experienced Cree interpreters in the North-West, could find no Cree equivalents for *traitor*, *rebellion*, or *crown*. When One Arrow heard himself accused of "knocking off the Queen's hat and stabbing her in the behind," he asked Houri, "Are you drunk?" However, a White man testified he saw One Arrow talking to Riel during the rebellion, so the chief was found guilty and sentenced to three years in Stony Mountain Penitentiary, Manitoba.

On August 17, Chief Poundmaker received the same sentence for the same charge, largely on the basis of a questionable letter sent to Riel with the chief's name written under it. Poundmaker, like the other chiefs, was not permitted to say one word in his own defence.

Big Bear had to wait until September 11 for his day in court. Two months locked inside log walls for a man who had lived his life outdoors and slept only inside the high cone of a buffalo-hide lodge—no wonder that, beyond the confusing charge, he appeared disoriented, hostile, old. And in the courtroom stood Peter Houri, who at Fort Walsh had interpreted Big Bear's long speech before he made his X mark in order to feed his starving People. They could only glance at each other, in silence.

There was no debate about nine White men being killed at Frog Lake, or Fort Pitt being sacked, or whether two hours of gunfire—perhaps three?—had been exchanged at

Frenchman Butte; the question was, had Big Bear been in command of the warriors when this violence happened? The court practice of translating only short summaries of testimony into Cree made it extremely difficult for Big Bear to follow the case against him, nor could he advise defence lawyer Beverly Robertson what answers to follow up on. Robertson, from Winnipeg, already had experience in defending both One Arrow and Poundmaker.

Robertson built his case around the fact that Big Bear was obliged to stay with his band in time of crisis, even when he strongly disagreed with his warriors' actions. Indeed, where else could an elderly Cree chief go?

John Pritchard testified that Big Bear had no control over the warriors at the Frog Lake killings, the shooting of Constable Cowan, or the destruction of Fort Pitt. James Simpson stated that at Frenchman Butte, Big Bear was two miles behind the rifle pits, that he had known the chief for "nearly forty years," and that he had "always been a good Indian to the white man." But now "his young men had succeeded in taking his good name from him." Company clerk Stanley Simpson (no relation to James) testified that he heard Big Bear say he wanted his men "to cut the head of the white people off," but Robertson quickly proved that Stanley understood no Cree, and certainly not such a complex statement. Catherine Simpson nervously murmured that Big Bear was in her kitchen when she heard the first shot fired at Frog Lake and that "he got up and went out, and I heard him say, don't do it … that is, leave it alone." William McLean, despite his two-month captivity, declared Big Bear to be "a good Indian," but he was no longer a leading man in the band, and that his son Imasees "treated him with utter contempt." The chief had neither taken nor accepted any pillaged goods at Fort Pitt, and during the councils on whether they should join Poundmaker, Big Bear "had no influence at that time [among] the leading spirits in the camp." Henry Halpin testified that Big Bear told him at Frog Lake that "this thing that has happened here was not my idea," and later that he "did not want to go toward Battleford," that is, join the rebels. Finally, William Cameron blurted out a long affirmation of the chief's good character, stating that in councils "Wandering Spirit did all the talking" and that it was Imasees—"one of the worst of the Indians and one of the headmen concerned in massacre"—who forced him to surrender all the ammunition in the Company store on April 2.

It seemed that, far from being guilty, Big Bear had done everything he could to prevent violence and murder. He had, in fact, saved many lives and continuously counselled peace.

Robertson, who had made a vigorous defence, considered the evidence for acquittal so strong that he ended his case. However, that a renowned head chief—who had, admittedly, done much good—could not leave his band during a severe crisis and would not have the power to control band warriors in times of starvation, rage, humiliation, battle-camaraderie, and attack remained incomprehensible to the all-White jury of Henry Grove, William Hunt, Robert Martin, John Morrison, Albert Smith, and J.W. Smith. They "return in fifteen minutes with a verdict of 'guilty,' with a recommendation to mercy."

Sentence was pronounced on September 25. Of the nineteen prisoners in the dock, Big Bear was called first. Judge Richardson asked, "Do you have anything to say before sentence is passed upon you?"

The man who once held audiences rapt for hours, whose voice of "amazing depth and volume" could "sound like the roar of a lion" and whose "gestures spoke almost as eloquently as his words" certainly had something to say. The hours of incomprehensible trial, where he was permitted nothing but silence, had not over-awed him. However, not one word of his speech appears in the official government record of his trial: 49 Victoria Sessional Papers (No.52) A. 1886. Only the *Toronto Mail* (October 5, 1885) printed a paraphrased summary, and it remained for Cameron, whose life Catherine Simpson had saved with a blanket, to offer some strands of memory. Forty years later he recreated some of the English translation in his personal memoir, *The War Trail of Big Bear*:

"The old man drew himself up with that imperious air that proclaimed him leader and fitted him so well.... He gave his head the little characteristic toss that always preceded his speeches.

"'I think I should have *something* to say,' he began slowly, 'about the occurrences which brought me here in *chains*.

"'I knew little of the killing at Frog Lake beyond hearing the shots fired. When any wrong was brewing, I did my best to stop it from the beginning. The turbulent ones of my band got beyond my control and shed the blood of those I would have protected. I was away from Frog Lake a part of the winter, hunting and fishing, and the rebellion had started before I got back. When white men were few in the country I gave them the hand of brotherhood. I am sorry so few are here who can witness to my friendly acts.

"'Can anyone stand here and say that I ordered the death of a priest or an agent? You think

I encouraged my people to take part in the trouble. I did not. I advised them against it. I felt sorry when they killed those men at Frog Lake, but the truth is when news of the fight at Duck Lake reached us, my band ignored my authority and despised me because I did not side with the half-breeds. I did not so much as take a white man's horse. I always believed that by being the friend of the white man, I and my people would be helped by those who had wealth. I always thought it paid to do all the good I could. Now my heart is on the ground.

"'I look around me in this room and see it crowded with handsome faces—faces far handsomer than mine (laughter). I have ruled my country for a long time. Now I am in chains, and will be sent to prison, but I have no doubt the handsome faces I admire will be competent to govern the land (laughter). At present I am dead to my people. Many of my band are hiding in the woods, paralyzed with terror. Cannot this court send them a pardon? My own children! Perhaps they are starving and outcast, too afraid to show themselves in the big light of day. If the government does not help them before winter, my band will surely perish.

"'But I have too much confidence in the Great Grandmother to fear that starvation will be allowed to overtake my people. The time will come when the Indians of the North-West will be of much service to the Great Grandmother. I plead again,' he cried, stretching forth his hands, 'to you, the chiefs of the white men's laws, for pity and help to the outcasts of my band!

"'I have only a few words more to say. Sometimes in the past I have spoken stiffly to the Indian agents, but when I did so it was only to obtain my rights. The North-West belonged to me, but I perhaps will not live to see it again. I ask the court to publish my speech and to scatter it among the white people. It is my defense.

"'I am old and ugly, but I have tried to do good. Pity the children of my tribe! Pity the old and helpless of my people! I speak with a single tongue; and because Big Bear has always been the friend of the white man, send out and pardon and give them help!

"'How! Aquisanee—I have spoken!'"

His speech, as he gave it in the court, was never published by the government "to scatter among the white people" so that any person who wished could read and remember it in the manner of the oral tradition. Not a word, neither as it was translated into English nor in Big Bear's Cree, has ever been found in any archive. And only one small newspaper—not even William Cameron in his memoir—documented the court's response. The *Regina Leader*, October 1, 1885, reported:

> "Judge Richardson ... told [Big Bear] that they never owned the land, that it belonged to the Queen, who allowed them to use it, that when she wanted to make other use of it She called them together through her officers and gave them the choicest portions of the country and that, as to his people, they would be looked after as though nothing had occurred. He was then sentenced to three years in the Penitentiary."

The land belongs to the Queen. From whom had she received it? The question Big Bear had always asked, and never heard an answer. Clearly, Richardson did not know, or had totally forgotten, that the Royal Proclamation by George III in 1763 spelled out the principle that indigenous people have an inalienable right to the lands they occupy, that the so-called "doctrine of right of discovery" in European international law was designed to control the competition among European nations themselves, and had no bearing on the relations those nations had with the Natives they "discovered" living on their land. As a free Cree man, Big Bear had always known he had an inalienable right to the land given him by the Great Spirit, but stating that fact with bitter irony in Richardson's courtroom helped him nothing. Poorly translated—or remembered—it only provoked shallow laughter.

And the judge's blithe statement that his People "would be looked after as though nothing had occurred," proved to be as much a lie as Morris's "you will still have the same mode of living as before."

Throughout the summer, Horsechild had been a sustaining comfort to Big Bear in prison. Mary PeeMee recounts:

> "The judge said to Big Bear, 'I cannot sentence your son to prison, but I can sentence him to residential school.' [The Battleford Industrial Residential School was organized in 1883 by Indian Affairs and the Anglican Church.] Then it was time to leave his father, and my man did not want to go. This was the first time he cried. Big

Bear talked to him for a long time. Then he took the medicine from around his neck and put it around the neck of Horsechild. Big Bear told him it would protect and guide him and he was never to take it off. Horsechild then left his father, and eventually came home."

From the context, it seems that this story concerns a necklace but Horsechild, later named Joe PeeMee, also received from his father the bear paw power bundle called Chief's Son's Hand. He cared for it for forty-nine years, until 1934, when at Little Pine Reserve he held a pipe ceremony and ritually presented the bundle to American anthropologist David Mandelbaum. Mandelbaum accepted the bundle, likely gave a gift of fifty dollars in return, and swore to keep it safe. PeeMee explained that he had many children and "there was no place for the bundle ... his main concern was finding a safe place for the medicine."

On October 13, 1934, Mandelbaum found a "safe place"; he deposited Chief's Son's Hand in the American Museum of Natural History, New York, where it has remained for three-quarters of a century. In 1988–89, a group of young Cree, including Jim Thunder and Lewis Cardinal, ran a Big Bear centenary pilgrimage on foot, four thousand three hundred kilometres from Edmonton to New York, to try to repatriate it. However, there was strong disagreement among Big Bear's descendants, both in Canada and Montana, as to where Chief's Son's Hand should go, and so museum officials refused to release it. In September 1994, curator Stanley Fried told me: "The American Museum will do the right thing [by the bundle], once we know what the right thing is. As long as the Cree cannot agree, it will stay here."

Today the bundle is no longer protected in PeeMee's original canvas bag; in fact, it is no longer a bundle. And it is no longer in a small room surrounded by hundreds of other communal Cree artifacts, the way I first saw it in June 1972. In November 2007, I found that all the museum's artifacts have been archived according to the materials of which they were made. Each of Chief's Son's Hand's nine wrapping cloths has been unleafed, numbered, and laid out separately. And I saw the ancient clawed paw as it had always been, sewn unevenly with leather thongs onto its red stroud by the Cree boy. But it now lies, numbered and naked, in a separate antiseptic drawer in the processed air of the huge museum vaults, with nothing but a twist of tobacco and a short braid of sweetgrass for companionship.

CHAPTER TWELVE

The Hills
of Sounding Lake

The Inmate Admittance Records at Stony Mountain
Penitentiary, Manitoba:

> "Prisoner # 103: Big Bear
> Term: 3 years
> Received: Sept. 29, 1885, from Regina
> Born: N.W.T.
> Age: 60
> Race: Native Canadian
> Married: Yes
> Religion: None
> Trade: None
> Height: 5' 5 1/4"
> Complexion: Dark
> Eyes and Hair: Black
> Crime: Treason Felony"

There was even less sunlight and air in Stony Mountain than in the police prison at Where The Bones Lie. The cell was not wood, and smaller, cut as it seemed out of piled limestone with iron bars for a door that opened into a black tunnel without windows. The stinking yellow light of coal oil. A mattress and a pail, and bells ten times a day.

"A.M.

5:50 Bell rings. Prisoners rise, wash, dress, make beds etc.

6:00 Bell rings. Prisoners unlocked, tubs emptied, etc.

6:45 Bell rings. Breakfast ready on stands. Prisoners marched to cell....

P.M.

6:00 Bell rings for locking up. Night Guard take charge of prison...."

The bell ruled. The brightest sun made no difference: there was always night in his cell. Forty-three of one hundred and ten inmates were People. One Arrow had to work mending White shoes; Big Bear began with carpentry, helping enlarge the prison, but eventually was assigned to clean pigpens. Poundmaker had been in Stony Mountain since August 21, 1885, and by Christmas he could barely walk for coughing. But once he and Big Bear met in the animal warmth of the barns.

Pigs stink, Big Bear said. If I'd known, I'd have eaten even less pork.

My young wife, liked bacon, Poundmaker whispered hoarsely. Some had good fat, to fry, potatoes.

Big Bear gestured to the guard, who nodded, and he touched Poundmaker's arm. Slowly they walked together into the sunlight, through the snow to Warden Sam Bedson's private zoo. His two bears were hidden in winter sleep, but his seven buffalo snuffled at hay in their wire pen.

Poundmaker whispered, Do you think, someday, they'll milk, them like cows?

The buffalo lifted their shaggy, expressionless heads to his Cree words. Big Bear felt so destroyed in this hateful place that he could only laugh; to speak would be weeping.

Journalists from Toronto and France came to have their pictures taken with "regal" Poundmaker, the only prisoner whose waist-long hair, by special dispensation, remained uncut. But the handsome chief was extremely ill, and for fear he would die in prison, he was discharged March 4, 1886. At about the same time thirty-one other Cree were released, including One Arrow, who only managed to reach St. Boniface before he died and was buried near Louis Riel in the cathedral cemetery. Poundmaker did reach home on the Battle River. Four months later he rode to his adoptive father Crowfoot at Blackfoot Crossing, and there he coughed his life out.

When Big Bear heard, he sought permission to visit the two bears. Their fur shone, they paced past each other inside their wire, rearing high like human beings at the corners and wheeling, dropping down to pace back again. Big Bear remembered his friend Poundmaker, only forty-four. He remembered his six Young Men hanged at the same instant in Battleford, every face, every laugh and cry of rage, every hand movement in warrior story: Iron Body; Little Bear; Bad Arrow; Round The Sky; Miserable Man; Wandering Spirit with his long hair white as snow. The rope torn into each broken neck.

Once, on Bull's Forehead Hill, the Great Parent of Bear had given him his vision, his bundle, his name, and also his power as a Cree boy, man, father, and chief. Now, when he should have been a respected Elder surrounded by his life's community, he stood alone, thrown away as a criminal. Watching two bears that were fed well enough—as he was— pacing the five steps of their White cage. Where had his life, his soul and spirit gone? Even in the open air, walls and wire multiplied around him. For a year he had not seen, unchained, the immense land he once rode over as easily as breathing. These poor bears, endlessly fed and forever imprisoned: despair threatened the very light of the sun. What he had seen while facing Morris at Pitt had come to pass, even for bears.

And calm gradually grew in him. Like the confidence he found when he was given *Iniskim* and offered it to the medicine stones above the Bow River. Trust the Buffalo—even when they disappear. Trust the Bear—even when they are imprisoned. As his body sickened in the cell shrinking around him, his spirit grew firmer. When, in January 1887, Mista-wasis and Ahtah-kakoop wrote to Dewdney, he was grateful to them despite their language.

> "We believe that Big Bear is the only Indian concerned in the rebellion remaining in prison ... and it would be very gratifying to the Cree nation if Her Majesty's Government would extend this criminal clemency...."

The prison doctor added his judicious word:

> "Prisoner 103 is very sick and rapidly getting worse ... his fainting spells are growing more frequent ... I would therefore urge most strongly that he be released as soon as possible."

On February 4, 1887, he was deemed fit to travel, and more than a month later, after enduring wagons and trains and freight carts, he was unloaded on the Little Pine Reserve. He had, of course, no reserve to return to.

Both the Poundmaker (#114) and Little Pine (#116) side-by-side reserves had been declared "DISLOYAL" in Assistant Indian Commissioner Hayter Reed's "List of Band Behaviour during Rebellion," and therefore their horses, guns, and carts had been taken from them; their treaty annuities cancelled for five years; and no one was allowed to leave either reserve without written permission from their agent. Their People existed below poverty. When Chief Thunderchild—his reserve also declared "DISLOYAL"—visited Big Bear, the dying chief finally spoke. "My heart is broken.... [In jail] I did the dirtiest work. One night I was placed in a bad place, a dungeon ... I hated it there, but I would not kill myself for I am not a coward. Now I will not last long.... My sons have gone to the States. I am alone."

The hundreds of Plains People who had once followed him as chief had scattered to whatever reserve would accept them; they feared government reprisals for any association with him. Though discharged, he remained a criminal, and he would never be allowed to choose a Big Bear Reserve to gather them together. Humiliation reached into his closest family: during his imprisonment his wife had begun to live with another man, and she refused to return. Horsechild, except for two months in summer, was locked in the industrial residential school at Battleford, and so Big Bear's daughter Earth Woman came from Montana to care for him.

The summer light, the poplar leaves flickering to a breeze in the Battle River valley, the ravines of Cutknife Hill blossoming white, turning purple with saskatoons, were beautiful to see. He leaned against the log wall of his cabin in the sun, watched thunderheads gather, and as winter approached he lay inside on his blankets. His spirit roamed over the long rivers and plains and valleys of his life, the lakes and hills of memory. But always he returned to Treaty Six, which Morris had brought and Sweetgrass had signed before they could discuss it: it never was read to him in Cree, and in all the years he had tried to talk, watch, argue, he had not been able to change any bit of what the Whites said was in it. And he returned to the one great unified "land set aside" he had envisioned for all the prairie People, to the delegation they would send to negotiate its boundaries and its conditions with the biggest White boss, wherever he might be. And how Dumont and Crozier shooting each other at Duck Lake had tipped Imasees and Wandering Spirit out of their frozen hatred into violence that destroyed all possibilities. Now Imasees and his families were trying to live in Montana on the garbage Whites threw away, and Wandering Spirit's family had scattered into northern forests—perhaps there the government would forget about them. And he … what was he, here beside this carefully measured barbed-wire fence strung between Little Pine and Poundmaker land?

Whites were truly amazing. They had more ropes than he had imagined when he told Morris that, just by seeing him, he felt one around his neck. And suddenly he recognized that this, too, was Bear's gift to him—an extremely sensitive neck! Big Bear laughed himself into a very nearly killing cough.

Ropes. To destroy a proud, independent people you made them sick, you wiped out their food, you took away their community, you made them afraid. Then you fenced them in on scattered bits of land, you didn't let them visit one another, you took their children and penned them up in schools like the ones near Battleford and Calgary, and you never let them come home or speak their language so you could never again tell them the sacred stories, nor listen to theirs.

Looking at Morris he had not thought of all that; his apprehension then had circled around being forced to accept the overwhelming White law. But now Whites had forced him to see "the rope" in their way, though there seemed no need for them to literally hang anyone. One Arrow and Poundmaker and very soon he himself would prove it: a three-year sentence in Stony Mountain was more than enough. The one difference: hanging was quicker.

Nevertheless, Horsechild had brought him the sacred bundle again, *That Which Is Kept In A Clean Place*. The mercy of The Great Spirit, the unfathomable goodness and power of the Great Parent of Bear remained. The buffalo and bear might be fenced in, like his People, but they would not die out. What he had done, what he had tried to do but failed to: the Creator's world remained and People belonged in it. His beloved People would not vanish, no matter what Whites forced upon them. They knew the place given them by the Creator because they knew the stories of this place, and they would live, raise their beautiful children, and a hundred years from now the sun and the moon would still shine upon them, the rivers run.

The government had used written treaties against his People, but perhaps, once they could understand and read and write the White words, they would be able to negotiate the treaties better. And perhaps, a century from now, the highest courts in Canada would come to recognize their magnificent traditions of oral memory, and they could begin talking about land and heritage and rights and living the way People talked. Talk, talk, they would keep on talking, make official apologies and act and talk some more. His insistence on talking to resolve conflict would become the Canadian way. They had, after all, named the whole country Canada, which sounded very much like the Cree word *kanâta*, meaning "the place that is clean."

Big Bear heard a powerful blizzard gathering itself around his cabin into a rising fury. He looked at Chief's Son's Hand, safely wrapped in a lifetime of gift cloths. He thought of the buffalo bursting from the water of Sounding Lake and running where they pleased over the prairie, of the bear whose tracks in the snow guided his family across the hills, south to the lodges of their People where the Red Deer River and the South Saskatchewan River flowed together in the great valleys below Bull's Forehead Hill.

BIG BEAR DIED at Poundmaker Reserve, Saskatchewan Territory, on January 17, 1888. He was buried on the snow-covered bluffs overlooking the Battle River. In August 1972, Elder John Tootoosis led me to the place. He said an Elder had shown him the grave in 1905 when he was six years old, and told him to remember.

1780s   Many Woods Cree and Saulteaux People begin to move out of the boreal forest and, over the next forty years, develop a tribal plains buffalo culture.

1795   The Hudson's Bay Company builds Forts Carlton and Edmonton for trade on the North Saskatchewan River.

1810–50   The Horse Wars develop on the prairies between the Plains Cree–Saulteaux allies and the Blackfoot Confederacy.

1825   Big Bear is born at Jackfish Lake (near present-day North Battleford, Saskatchewan).

1829   The Hudson's Bay Company builds Fort Pitt.

1832–33   Famine spreads among North Saskatchewan Plains Cree.

1837   Lower and Upper Canada rebellions take place.

1838   A smallpox epidemic breaks out among prairie People. Big Bear survives but is badly scarred.

1838–39   Big Bear goes on a vision quest on Bull's Forehead Hill.

1841   Chief Maskepetoon, a Cree peace advocate, is
            baptized by Methodist Robert Rundle.

1845–47   Major battles take place between Plains Cree and
            Blackfoot; Big Bear is a leading young warrior.

LATE 1840s Big Bear marries Sayos. Their daughter
            Nowakich and son Twin Wolverine are born.

1850–1870   The Horse Wars intensify into the Buffalo
            Wars between the Plains Cree–Saulteaux allies
            and the Blackfoot Confederacy.

1851   Big Bear's son Imasees is born. In Canada, the
            Baldwin-LaFontaine "Great Ministry" achieves
            responsible government.

1856   John A. Macdonald becomes joint premier of
            the Province of Canada.

1864–65   Severe measles epidemics strike the Cree.
            Scarlet fever breaks out among Blackfoot.

1864   The Charlottetown Conference begins the
            process of Canadian Confederation.

1865   Big Bear's father, Chief Black Powder, dies. Big
            Bear is chosen chief of his band.

1866   The Iron Stone, "Old Man Buffalo," is stolen
            from a hilltop near the Battle River.

1867   On July 1, the Confederation of four provinces
        creates Canada. John A. Macdonald becomes the
        first prime minister.

1869   On November 19, Canada "buys" Rupert's Land
        from the Hudson's Bay Company for $1.5 million.

        On December 8, Louis Riel declares a provisional
        government at Red River.

1869–70 Smallpox devastates the prairie People.
        Maskepetoon is killed by the Blackfoot.

1870   On May 12, Canada declares Manitoba a province.
        Canadian militia force Riel to flee to the United
        States.

        In October, the last, and largest, battle between
        Plains Cree and Blackfoot is fought on the
        Oldman River.

1871   The Plains Cree chiefs, including Big Bear,
        write a letter to Canada from Fort Edmonton:
        "We heard our lands were sold and we did
        not like it.…"

1871–77 Canada concludes seven treaties with all
        Aboriginal Peoples from Lake of the Woods to the
        Rocky Mountains.

1873   A confrontation takes place between Big Bear and
        Métis Gabriel Dumont over buffalo hunting.

1873   Macdonald resigns due to the Pacific Scandal.
        Alexander Mackenzie becomes prime minister.

1874   The North West Mounted Police march west
        from Red River and build Fort Macleod on the
        Oldman River.

1875   Reverend George McDougall carries treaty mes-
        sages to the prairie Cree. He reports that Big Bear
        is "a most troublesome fellow."

1875   The North West Mounted Police build Fort
        Calgary on the Bow River.

1876   The Cree and Lieutenant-Governor Morris sign
        Treaty Six at Fort Carlton and Fort Pitt; Big Bear,
        who was not invited, arrives late and refuses to
        sign without more consultation.

1877   No government official comes to discuss Treaty
        Six with Big Bear. The Blackfoot Confederacy
        signs Treaty Seven at Blackfoot Crossing.

1878   Big Bear tells Lieutenant-Governor Laird that he
        will live by the hunt for four years while he
        observes how Canada treats treaty People living
        on reserves.

1878   Macdonald is re-elected. He will remain prime
        minister and head of Indian Affairs until his
        death in 1891.

1879   The last buffalo vanish from the Canadian prairie.

        Macdonald names Edgar Dewdney Indian
        Commissioner of the North-West Territories.

1879–82 Big Bear's band—grown to more than two
        thousand members—hunt the last buffalo in
        Montana. In Canada, treaty People try to learn
        farming, but scattered reserve life is a starvation
        disaster.

1881   Macdonald names Edgar Dewdney Lieutenant-
        Governor as well as Indian commissioner.

1882   Harassed by the U.S. Army, Big Bear's huge band
        returns to Canada. On December 8, he signs his
        adhesion to Treaty Six at Fort Walsh.

1883   Big Bear's reduced band is forced to live in the
        Fort Pitt–Frog Lake area.

1884   In June, Big Bear gives a Thirst Dance. A face-off
        with the police almost explodes into killing.

        In July, Gabriel Dumont brings Louis Riel back
        from Montana to Batoche.

In August, Big Bear convinces the Cree chiefs to speak "with one voice" to the government.

1884–85   While wintering at Frog Lake, Big Bear plans negotiations with the government for one huge reserve for all the Plains People.

1885   On March 19, Riel declares the Métis Provisional Government of the Saskatchewan at Batoche.

On March 29, the Battle of Duck Lake takes place between Métis and the North West Mounted Police.

On April 2, warriors from Big Bear's band kill nine White men at Frog Lake.

On April 15, the Frog Lake Cree capture and sack Fort Pitt.

On May 12, Canadian militia overrun Batoche and capture Riel; Dumont escapes.

On May 28, the Cree battle Canadian militia until both retreat at Frenchman Butte.

On June 3, Militia scatter the Cree into flight at Loon Lake Crossing.

On July 2, Big Bear surrenders to police near Carlton.

On July 20, Riel's trial for treason begins at Regina; on August 1, he is sentenced to hang.

On September 11, Big Bear goes on trial for treason-felony. He is found guilty.

On September 25, Big Bear is sentenced to three years in Stony Mountain Penitentiary.

On November 16, Louis Riel is hanged at Regina.

On November 27, eight Aboriginal men, six from Big Bear's band, are hanged at Battleford.

1887 In January, Big Bear is gravely ill; he is discharged from Stony Mountain Penitentiary and reaches the Little Pine Reserve in March.

1888 On January 17, Big Bear dies on the Poundmaker Reserve.

1916 Imasees (Little Bear) and his band are finally granted a reservation, at Rocky Boy, near Havre, Montana.

SOURCES

Cameron, William. *The War Trail of Big Bear* (Toronto: Ryerson, 1926).

Campbell, Maria. "She Who Knows the Truth of Big Bear," *Maclean's*, September 1975.

Canada. Sessional Papers (No. 52), 1886, 49 Victoria, "Queen vs. Big Bear," pp. 172–233.

Christensen, Deanna. *Ahtahkakoop* (Shell Lake, SK: Ahtahkakoop Publishing, 2000).

Dempsey, Hugh. *Big Bear: The End of Freedom* (Vancouver: Douglas & McIntyre, 1984).

Fine Day. *My Cree People* (Invermere, BC: Good Medicine Books, 1973).

Fraser, William. *Big Bear, Indian Patriot* (Calgary: Historical Society of Alberta, 1966).

Light, Douglas. *Footprints in the Dust* (North Battleford, SK: Turner-Warwick Publications, 1987).

Little Bear, Isabelle. "My Own Story." *Bonnyville Tribune* (AB), April–May 1958.

Mandelbaum, David. *The Plains Cree* (New York: American Museum of Natural History, 1940).

McLean, William. Reminiscences of the Tragic Events at Frog Lake and in Fort Pitt District with Some of the Experiences of the Writer and His Family during the North-West Rebellion of 1885. Copy received from Duncan McLean, Winnipeg, 1971.

McLeod, Neal. "Rethinking Treaty Six in the Spirit of Mistahi Maskwa (Big Bear)," *The Canadian Journal of Native Studies*, XIX, 1 (1999): 68–89.

Morris, Alexander. *The Treaties of Canada with the Indians of Manitoba and the North-West Territories* (Belfords, Clarke & Co., 1880; reprint, Coles, 1971).

O-sak-do. Treaty No. 6 Centennial Commemoration Tabloid (Saddle Lake, AB: Saddle Lake Reserve, July 1976).

Saskatchewan Herald. Battleford, North-West Territories, 1878–1888.

Sluman, Norma, and Jean Goodwill. *John Tootoosis* (Ottawa: Golden Dog Press, 1982).

Stonechild, Blair, and Bill Waiser. *Loyal till Death: Indians and the North-West Rebellion* (Calgary: Fifth House, 1997).